THRU-HIKING THE AT

A SUMMER OF ADVENTURE ON THE APPALACHIAN TRAIL

RYAN HOUSER

Copyright © 2019 RYAN HOUSER

All rights reserved.

ISBN: 9781708783020

To anyone crazy enough to actually consider following all those white blazes.

CONTENTS

Foreword

1. The AT and Planning — 1
2. The Southern Mountains — 6
3. The Mid Atlantic — 49
4. New England — 112
5. Katahdin — 184

About the Author — 188

FOREWORD

I know what you're thinking, "How incredibly original, another book about the Appalachian Trail… Why is this book different from any of the other countless books on the AT?" That's a good question, and one that I had myself before putting this together. For starters, I took incredibly detailed notes during my thru hike, more so than any hiker I've met. I originally wrote them for myself and family that were following along, but I have decided to share them with people who may find them helpful or inspiring. Secondly, this book is intended for those who want to know what it is really like to thru hike the Appalachian Trail, or those that may be considering a thru hike of their own. It's for those who might have let the notion of a five-month long backpacking trip enter their mind and suddenly find themselves constantly daydreaming about planning and executing such a trip. If this is happening to you, you'll know it. I knew it when it was happening to me. It consumed me for over a year before I left.

Here's what this book is not: It's not a manual for how to thru hike the Appalachian Trail. It's also not intended as pure entertainment in the typical sense. If you are looking for a book brimming with satire or comedic Appalachian trivia, this isn't it. There are no film-adaptations forthcoming. I might suggest a copy of Bill Bryson's A Walk in the Woods. It was one of the first books I picked up when I first learned of the trail. It's brilliant, funny and educational all at once.

If however, you want to know what it's really like to complete the Appalachian Trail, something Bryson did not, this book is for you. It's simply the day-to-day encounters, thoughts, adjacent adventures and journal entries of a young hiker in the summer of 2012 who set out from Georgia with a pack, a few necessities, some food and a newfound desire to challenge themselves.

Keep in mind that many of my entries were written from my sleeping bag with heavy eyes after a 30 mile day in the mountains. I was also just a young college graduate at the time of the trip. I have refrained from editing as much as possible in an attempt to preserve my original experiences and thoughts. The trail also changes from year to year. If you are planning a section or thru hike, be sure to consult a current guidebook or a mobile app for planning your travel. I didn't use a phone app on my thru hike but they have now changed the way hikers engage with the trail.

CHAPTER 1: THE AT AND PLANNING

The AT

The Appalachian Trail is seemingly never ending. At least that's how it feels when you've hiked through ice, pounding rain, sweltering heat, over mountain after mountain, some with switch-backs, some without, for over 1,000 miles, and then come to the realization that you're not even halfway through. The trail begins in the heart of the south at Springer Mountain in Georgia, winding its way up by Washington DC, past New York, all the way to New England and into central Maine, with a grand finale at Mt. Katahdin at Baxter State Park.

The trail was approximately 2,184 miles the year of my attempt. The length varies from year to year, but tends to increase with added mileage from yearly trail maintenance efforts. Those who attempt to complete the trail in a single season are called "thru-hikers". In the past only 10% to 15% of those who make the attempt actually finish. Some statistics show that this number is getting closer to a 25% completion rate. Maybe it's the lighter gear, or the online planning resources, or people writing books like this one. Whatever the reason, the fact still stands that most people who attempt a thru hike don't succeed.

In total the trail passes through 14 states (this was more states than I had been to in my life up until the point I hiked the AT) including Georgia, North Carolina, Tennessee, Virginia, West Virginia, Maryland, Pennsylvania, New Jersey, New York, Connecticut, Massachusetts, Vermont, New Hampshire, and Maine. Most of the trail is wilderness, although many portions pass through towns, along roads both paved and unpaved, and cross bridges.

Thru-hikers starting in Georgia and hiking north are called north-bounders, or NOBO's. Those attempting a southbound hike are referred to as SOBO's. Some folks flip flop, often to avoid looming fall weather, which entails hiking half of the trail, then shuttling to the end and hiking back to the halfway point. It can take anywhere from three to six months to complete a thru-hike. Professional runners with support and fastpackers with experience have done it in less than two months. It took me 108 days, which might not seem fast compared to those records, but it's faster than average for an unsupported thru hike. There are many towns close to the trail that provide resupply. Most hikers carry two to four days of food at a time.

It's a misconception that most thru-hikers tent out every night on the AT. I actually spent most of my nights on trail in three-walled shelters. There are approximately 200 shelters along the AT. I loved shelters on my hike. Their quirks and comforts provided physical and mental refuge from the rugged terrain and weather. Eventually they started to feel like my home. I stayed in them almost exclusively except for one stretch in the mid Atlantic where mosquitoes were out in droves. This offered me several benefits: Shelters are usually close to water sources, it's a good way to meet other hikers if you are hiking solo as I did, and, most importantly, it helped me avoid setting up my tent and dealing with it when it's inevitably wet in the morning. Likewise, avoiding shelters and tenting out is a good option if a hiker prefers more solitude.

The remaining narration of this book will be turned over to my former self several years ago as I prepared for and eventually hiked the entire AT in 2012.

Planning: There Was An Attempt

Start Date: April 29th, Approach Trail

Direction: Northbound, Georgia to Maine

Base Pack Weight: 9.5 lbs

Trail Name: To Be Determined

I've been planning and researching for this hike for almost two years now. I'm graduating college soon and that means my opportunity has finally come.

There's a few reasons I'm doing it: It seems like an enormous physical and mental challenge. It will give me an opportunity to travel and meet new and interesting people. I will get to re-acquaint myself with the nature I experienced as a child. It will give me an introspective period of personal reflection and a chance to push my mind and body to see what I'm really made of.

In short, and for now anyway, long-distance backpacking appeals to me; I know it doesn't to some. I find the thought of carrying the bare essentials that I need to live on my back an inviting notion after being subject to university cultures for so long, where the social and academic expectations dominate my night and day. I'm ready to experience something completely different, real and outside of my comfort zone.

      I am starting alone but I expect to meet and form friendships with many other thru-hikers, old and young, who are also attempting this trek. Based on my current pack weight I can describe my backpacking style as "ultra-light", or "UL" as it's abbreviated in the industry. I know there are physical benefits to carrying as little as possible, but there also seems to be some mental benefits as well. If I'm doing everything I possibly can to make reaching Maine easier, maybe I will beat the odds. Every former thru hiker I've talked to has suggested cutting everything from my pack but the bare essentials, and I'm trying my best to heed their advice.

CHAPTER 2: THE SOUTHERN MOUNTAINS

Southern terminus plaque, AT Mile 0

Day 1

Location: Stover Creek Shelter

AT mile: 2.8

Miles hiked today: 11.3

Dad dropped me off at Amicalola Falls State Park around 1:30 pm and I registered at the infor mation center as thru hiker number 996 for this year. I did the 8.5 mile approach trail much faster than I anticipated. The stairs were just as hard as everyone warned they would be. At the top I took a photo with the southern terminus plaque, then made it 2.8 miles north to this shelter. Wildlife abounds already, as I encountered a chipmunk, turkey and snake in just this half day of hiking. Dad is camping with me for tonight with his new puppy, which is comforting and eases my nerves. He met me at the first road intersection north of the southern terminus. They will be leaving me on my own tomorrow.

Two of the hikers at our shelter have guitars and we have a fire going. I talked them into letting Dad play and they were impressed with his Doc Watson style finger picking even though he was a little rusty. I have no signal in this valley so I'm going to post this up tomorrow. Making this entry short so I can be sociable on my first night.

Day 2

Location: Woody Gap

AT mile 21.2

Miles hiked: 18.4

I didn't intend on going this far today but I arrived at Gooch Mountain Shelter at 1:30 pm where I had originally planned to stay for the night, so I decided to hike on. Dad left me this morning and headed south back to the parking lot and I headed north around 7:30 am.

This morning I came to a footbridge where a massive white stray dog was wandering about. If it was black it could have passed as a bear. No owner in sight. He followed me a few miles before leaving the trail. I took a 30 minute nap alone at Gooch Mountain Shelter because I was feeling beat, unseasoned. I rested there on my back on the shelter floor in a puddle of my own sweat beginning to question my decision to start this trip.

These GA mountains are known to be tough. They don't have as many switchbacks as I am used to on other sections of the AT that I have done previously. I met two older guys that are hiking to NC. I also met two girls who got a hitch into town from Woody Gap just before sunset. I've decided to tent out here tonight and shoot for Neels Gap tomorrow where I may get a bunk. Tomorrow I cross the Blood Mountain Wilderness area where bears have been stealing hiker's food bags. They are enforcing a bear canister only rule for camping there so I'm trying to push through it and not stop for the night.

The logistics of avoiding that area is another reason I pushed on today. I had dinner with an awesome view to the southeast from Woody Gap. It seemed to make my Knor Pasta Sides taste a lot better. I think I'll go to bed early tonight so I can recover from these 18 miles. I still lack a trail name, but there's no need to rush I guess.

I did see my first bear today. A small black cub that scampered away on a fallen tree as I hiked by, about 15 feet away. No mom in sight. It disappeared as I was trying to get the camera out. I spotted it only about 200 yards from a bear activity warning sign. I've never seen one in the wild before and I never thought I would see one this early. An awesome conclusion to a full day.

Day 3

Location: Whitley Gap Shelter

AT mile: 38.4

Miles hiked today: 17.2

Left out early this morning and made it over Blood Mountain by noon. Really rewarding views up there with a two-room stone shelter. Met a thru hiker named Keith from Alabama who is 33 years old. I hiked with him down to Neels Gap. At the outfitter there I charged my phone, picked up some resupply and had a glorious hot dog.

Made it to Whitley Gap Shelter which is 1.2 miles off the AT. Didn't want to do the extra 2.4 out and back but I was too tired and hungry to go any farther. I hiked in the rain for a bit today but only a few light showers. Looks like I may stop in Hiawasee GA the night after next for a hostel since I skipped the one at Neels. That means hopefully by Friday I'll reach my home state, the NC border.

Water hasn't been too difficult to find and purify but I was running low at one point today when it was the hottest out. I bet I've been drinking eight liters of water a day and I still feel a little dehydrated. I wake up in the middle of the night wanting more. Not sure where I'm headed tomorrow but I will try to post again if I have signal.

Day 4

Location: Tray Mountain Shelter

AT mile: 58.6

Miles hiked today: 20.2

HUGE day today and I'm feeling it now. First 20+ mile day of the trip and some of the hardest terrain yet. Last night was eventful, the shelter was infested with mice. I bet I saw eight and heard a dozen more. One crawled across another guy and it must have shook him up a bit. He went outside and slept on top of the picnic table. One jumped in my dry bag and I had to run him out. Not sure why because there wasn't any food in it. I think they are just conditioned to go after any bags in sight.

Two other wildlife-related incidents happened today. I saw yet another bear, this one about half grown and on the actual trail in front of me. It saw me and ran down the trail away from me and into the woods. I also got my first tick today. It hadn't bit me luckily. An estimated 5% of thru hikers get Lyme Disease from ticks, usually north of VA but it can happen anywhere.

Met a guy from Israel at Blue Mountain Shelter where I stopped for lunch. He was about my age and had come to the US to hike the AT. I rolled into Tray Mountain Shelter around 4 pm expecting it to be empty but there are 12 others here. Four of the guys I talked to are thru hiking. I've decided to tent out again tonight since the shelter is packed.

Tomorrow I think I will hitch a ride into Hiawasee and get some real food, a shower and a bed. That's right, I haven't had a shower yet. Also need to wash some clothes. Definitely the hardest day yet. If everything goes as planned I'll be finished with my first state by Friday.

Hitchhiking

Day 5

Location: Hiawassee, GA

AT mile: 69.6

Miles hiked today: 11

    The last 24 hours have been like a dream. Last night I slept at an elevation of 4,200 feet, the highest I've camped on the AT yet. It was the first night I was glad to have my sleeping bag. I met a young photographer who ended up making her hammock only a few feet from my tent. She thru hiked the whole trail last year and was just out now to photograph. We stayed up late talking about her thru. She told me some good spots to see sunsets in NC.

I got up around 6:15 am to a pink sunrise and a giant cloud behind us. Looking over the side of the mountain was a solid wall of white, like there was nothing below us. I broke camp and started hiking north for Dick's Creek Gap. I reached the road crossing at the gap around noon and as soon as I sat my pack down and started hitching for a ride into Hiawassee, a couple in the parking lot came up and offered me a ride. They were very generous and even drove me through the town to show me everything before dropping me off at the Hiawassee Inn.

I checked in, took a shower, washed my clothes and dried my tent and tarp out in the parking lot from last night's condensation. Since I don't have an extra set of clothes I was walking around the parking lot in a towel while my clothes washed (this would turn into a town-day attire ritual) . This place has that kind of vibe though, because everybody I've seen at this inn are hikers and some are part of the crew I met last night at the shelter.

It's strange being in a town without a car. I walked to Hardee's for lunch. What's an extra mile after walking almost 80? I stayed off the sidewalk and on the grass because it was softer on my feet.

It's also strange to have clean running water after having to purify everything I drink from streams.

I stopped by an outfitter to get more denatured alcohol for my stove. The lady there told me to get what I needed and leave a donation, which I did. Everybody I've encountered here is so genuine and nice. I resupplied on food at Ingles. Dried macaroni and cheese, dried fruit, summer sausage, ramen, milky ways and butterfingers, Slim Jims and beef jerky, granola bars, raisins, dried mashed potatoes, Cheez Its, grits and trail mix. That should last me the next few days until I can get into Franklin.

I want to thank everybody who has been sending me text messages of encouragement. They really do pick me up when it gets tough. Weather is looking like a decent chance of thunderstorms for the weekend so hopefully this night in a bed will energize me and help me to stay strong. I can't wait to hit the Nantahala Outdoor Center, get some views from the fire towers near there, see some of the giant grassy balds of NC and push on up into the Great Smoky Mountains National Park. GA has been fun but I know firsthand how beautiful the mountains of NC and TN can be.

young photographer who ended up making her hammock only a few feet from my tent. She thru hiked the whole trail last year and was just out now to photograph. We stayed up late talking about her thru. She told me some good spots to see sunsets in NC.

I got up around 6:15 am to a pink sunrise and a giant cloud behind us. Looking over the side of the mountain was a solid wall of white, like there was nothing below us. I broke camp and started hiking north for Dick's Creek Gap. I reached the road crossing at the gap around noon and as soon as I sat my pack down and started hitching for a ride into Hiawassee, a couple in the parking lot came up and offered me a ride. They were very generous and even drove me through the town to show me everything before dropping me off at the Hiawassee Inn.

I checked in, took a shower, washed my clothes and dried my tent and tarp out in the parking lot from last night's condensation. Since I don't have an extra set of clothes I was walking around the parking lot in a towel while my clothes washed (this would turn into a town-day attire ritual) . This place has that kind of vibe though, because everybody I've seen at this inn are hikers and some are part of the crew I met last night at the shelter.

It's strange being in a town without a car. I walked to Hardee's for lunch. What's an extra mile after walking almost 80? I stayed off the sidewalk and on the grass because it was softer on my feet.

It's also strange to have clean running water after having to purify everything I drink from streams.

I stopped by an outfitter to get more denatured alcohol for my stove. The lady there told me to get what I needed and leave a donation, which I did. Everybody I've encountered here is so genuine and nice. I resupplied on food at Ingles. Dried macaroni and cheese, dried fruit, summer sausage, ramen, milky ways and butterfingers, Slim Jims and beef jerky, granola bars, raisins, dried mashed potatoes, Cheez Its, grits and trail mix. That should last me the next few days until I can get into Franklin.

I want to thank everybody who has been sending me text messages of encouragement. They really do pick me up when it gets tough. Weather is looking like a decent chance of thunderstorms for the weekend so hopefully this night in a bed will energize me and help me to stay strong. I can't wait to hit the Nantahala Outdoor Center, get some views from the fire towers near there, see some of the giant grassy balds of NC and push on up into the Great Smoky Mountains National Park. GA has been fun but I know firsthand how beautiful the mountains of NC and TN can be.

Southern mountains and a wall of clouds

Day 6

Location: Standing Indian Shelter

AT Mile: 86.3

Miles hiked today: 16.7

    My hitch out of Hiawassee wasn't as easy as my hitch in. It took me 30 minutes to get a ride. Most drivers seemed like they were rushing to work. I did figure this much out: the lady wearing the sunglasses driving the white BMW is not picking you up while you're standing in the rain.

    On a more positive note I made it to North Carolina today. Hitting the NC/GA sign felt like I had suddenly arrived in my backyard. I met a retired electrical engineer named Patrick from TN today and hiked most of the way with him to this shelter. He's hiking to VA.

Didn't sweat near as much today. The early morning rain cooled everything off. It actually seemed like my easiest hiking day yet. Maybe because I was going at a slower pace while hiking with others, or maybe it was just their company distracting me. I got lunch today by the famously photographed twisted tree just beyond the NC state line. I have seen so many pictures of it prior to my hike.

Three older guys are staying at the shelter with me tonight, all hiking solo. One has a trail name of Spirit Walker. They are an interesting bunch, and all have a great sense of humor that only ten old guys in the woods together could have. Expecting some amazing views from Standing Indian Mountain tomorrow from what I hear. Goodnight from NC!

Day 7

Location: Winding Stair Gap (Franklin, NC)

AT Mile: 109.8

Miles hiked today: 23.5

Today has been like no other thus far. I realized I needed to refill my denatured alcohol in Franklin but the outfitter there is closed on Sunday, so I made a huge push down to Winding Stair Gap in hopes of catching them today. For the first time in my adult life I had completely forgotten it was the weekend. I knew something was up when more hikers than usual were on the trail.

I hit the 100 mile mark today. I feel pretty good even after a 23+ mile day. The feet are a little sore. It was extremely windy this morning. I was above 5,000 ft in elevation for the first time. Trees were whipping and creaking above my and another day hiker's head and it made us a little uneasy.

When I hit the fire tower at Albert Mountain a large group of older day hikers arrived in from the north. They were interested in my thru hike and offered me cold, fresh strawberries. Just what I needed. When I got to winding stair gap I began to try and hitch 10 miles east into Franklin. A couple walked off the trail behind me and offered a ride. I rode in the back of their truck's cab with their adopted Golden Retriever Ted. They dropped me off at the outfitter. I got more fuel and asked the guy if there was anywhere I could tent out. He called the manager and said it was fine if I pitched in their grass. They even let me charge my camera and phone. Before bed I walked to a nearby Huddle House and devoured some breakfast food. My tent is across the road from a Lowes and McDonald's and next to a Sonic, not a potential camping spot I had imagined when I was planning my hike. It's not quite visible to cars because it's elevated but I never would have thought I would be able to see the golden arches from my tent on my thru hike…

While resupplying I picked up a breakfast bar, read "only 90 calories" and threw it back into the bin. I'm trying to consume as many calories as possible and no matter how hard I try I'll still burn that off.

I enjoy many of the older guys I've met on trail. The young ones like to talk about gear and doing miles and why their setup is best, etc. The older crowd is more entertaining. They seem to respect me a lot. One told me he could tell I have discipline. It's true that I'm always hiking by 7:30 am where many younger guys seem to sleep in.

There are all kinds on the trail. Many thru-hikers have a different philosophy than me. They will skip a tough section, or "yellow blaze" i.e. hitch a ride farther north to meet back up with a group or avoid a difficult stretch. It seems I've adopted the strategy of the purist. I want to hike every foot of the trail. That means if I take a side trail to a shelter, I don't take a different side trail back to the the AT farther north. I retrace my steps to where I left the AT and begin from there. Of course there's no right or wrong way to hike, and "hike your own hike" still stands. This is just the approach I want to take. I'm here to hike the AT, so that's what I'm going to do.

Day 8

Location: Wesser Bald Shelter

AT mile: 131.4

Miles hiked today: 21.6

Started walking down highway 64 this morning out of Franklin and got a ride by a lady on the way to a day hike. She dropped me off at Winding Stair Gap and I headed north. I met a couple from Connecticut who were section hiking and live just off the trail. They gave me their information and told me to call them if I make it up that far and they will give me a place to stay. That's the third time somebody from farther north has extended this offer.

Dark clouds and thunder hung around most of the day and it rained for maybe an hour. I crossed my first few balds today and the lightning had me nervous above tree line. At Wayah Bald I met a giant group of boy scouts, all about 12 years old that took an interest in my hike.

I had planned on only doing 15 miles today and staying at Cold Springs Shelter but when I arrived it was full. Not wanting to deal with a wet tent for the second night in a row I pushed farther to Wesser Bald Shelter. There are six of us here, four thru hikers and one section hiker. We will all hit the NOC tomorrow for hot showers and laundry. I've been to the NOC before to hike so tomorrow will be the first time I reach a point on the AT that I have actually hiked on before.

Day 9

Location: NOC (Nantahala Outdoor Center)

AT Mile: 137.3

Miles hiked today: 5.9

      Taking a nero (near zero mile day) to rest up after hiking about 50 miles since Saturday morning. Had a huge descent today to get down from an elevation drop nicknamed "The Jump Off" to the rafting center at the Nantahala river. I saw my first venomous snake today, a copperhead curled up inside an old hollow stump.

      Everybody always thinks of the ascents as being the most difficult part of hiking. I would agree that they are the most strenuous, but the descents are the most painful. Those are the ones that you feel in your knees, joints and feet.

      I checked into the bunk house for hikers here and I'm sharing a four bunk room with two other hikers I met last night. I took a cool shower and washed my clothes. I got lunch at a restaurant on the river with a thru hiker and section hiker. The section hiker, trail named Rogue, just finished his last southern section of the AT. He has been at it for over ten years and today has completed everything up to Vermont, something like 1500 miles.

      I picked up some aluminum foil from the hiker box in the outfitter here to use over my cooking pot to hopefully decrease my water boiling time.

A hiker box is where hikers can dump things they don't need or are tired of carrying. Everything from pre-packaged food to gear to you name it can be found in one and it's all up for grabs.

I can't believe that in another two days I will be entering the Great Smoky Mountains National Park. The highest point on the entire AT is in the park at Clingman's Dome. It looks like temperatures might drop some by then so i will probably see some nights in the 30's. I've always dreamed of hiking all the way through the Smokies and now I finally get to do it. I've found that's how you have to approach the days out here. You can't think of it as hiking to Maine. I can't even conceive of hiking that far. You have to think of it as a series of three day hikes strung together. I set my goals on the next town, the next resupply point, the next landmark or checkpoint, and I just focus on getting to there.

I've met so many people from all over the US. Utah, Florida, Colorado, it's always strange when I say I'm from NC while we're in NC. Tomorrow I have a massive ascent so I'm going to try and hit the trail early so I can make Fontana Dam in two days.

Boom Boom, a name given to one of the section hikers I ran into at the NC border and spent a night with in the Standing Indian Shelter, rolled into the NOC right at sunset. It was like seeing an old friend even though I only spent part of a day with him. I love how close the trail community is.

Everybody looks out for one another, shares food, helps each other out. The guys that are 40 or 50 years old treat me like I'm their best friend. It's truly a community completely separated from society, with its own set of unspoken understandings. I see why many prefer this lifestyle over what we're used to.

Mando on a foggy early morning ascent

Day 10

Location: Brown Fork Gap Shelter

AT mile: 153.1

Miles hiked today: 16

I climbed over 5,000 ft today, over 3,000 by 9:30 am. It was really foggy on the ascent until about noon. Now it has turned into a beautiful afternoon and the sun is shining. The weather in the mountains changes fast. I ran into Patrick aka Mando (he's a fantastic mandolin player and carries one in his pack) and hiked with him for most of the day. He's one of the few older hikers that can do 18+ mile days.

I don't know if it was the early climb or the lack of good sleep in the bunkhouse last night but I felt groggy this morning and throughout the first half of the day. Headache and my pack is digging into my shoulders more. I think I've lost some weight and my hip belt is pulled as tight as it will go so more pack weight is being distributed on my shoulders. I need to find something to duct tape inside the belt to make it smaller.

Luckily when we hit NC 143 today there was trail magic waiting for us by the pull off. After a few Little Debbie's and a Mountain Dew I was feeling much better. I think partly from just getting my first trail magic. I've heard so much about it in the past but never experienced it.

Another hiker named Ben is staying with us at the shelter tonight. He is at school at Appalachian State so he's going as far north as he can before August. I had thought about doing that last year while I was still enrolled, but I'm glad I've waited for the opportunity to do the whole trail without a time commitment.

Mando played his mandolin this evening as we made dinner at the shelter. He plays in a band and he's really good with it. It's nice to hear music that's authentic and natural. One young guy behind us was actually hiking with a full-size banjo but i don't think we'll see him much anymore. Full-size banjo's seem to slow folks down.

We hit a steep ascent today just before the shelter nicknamed "Jacob's Ladder". Mando was struggling and I was out of breath. You know a climb is going to be tough when it has its own nickname, and many on the AT do. Rogue from Utah told me if the guidebook shows an elevation gain of 700+ feet in less than a mile, you're in for a tough ascent.

Ben is tenting out tonight so there are only two of us in the eight-person shelter, so I think I will get better sleep. Tomorrow we reach Fontana Dam. The trail actually crosses the top of the dam before entering the Smokies. I have to get a thru hiker permit to hike through the Smokies. Regulations inside the park are fairly strict and they don't hesitate to fine you for stepping out of line. I won't actually enter the Smokies until Thursday. Tomorrow night I plan to stay at the Fontana Dam shelter that sleeps up to 24 people. It's enormous, they call it the Fontana Hilton. There are even showers in it. Showers in an AT shelter, it's hard for me to wrap my head around it.

Day: 11

Location: Fontana Dam Shelter (aka the Fontana Hilton)

AT mile: 165.8

Miles hiked today: 12.7

Hiked down to Fontana this morning and got really wet. Thick fog through the first half of the morning and steady rain through the second half. Hiking through clouds gets you soaked even without rain. The condensation clings to your skin and clothes until eventually you are just drenched. Typing this from my iPhone in the shelter now trying to dry everything out.

When I hit the first road before the dam I got a shuttle with a few other young hikers that were trying to go into Fontana Village. I resupplied at the general store there and got two hot dogs for lunch.

I got dropped off and hiked back down to the Fontana Hilton. There is a shower house next to it and about ten people already in the shelter. I filled out the paper register as a thru hiker for a Great Smoky Mountains backcountry permit. Everybody has to have one to enter the park. One of the guys here found a four leaf clover outside and gave it to me for good luck.

I think I'm going to try and do the Smokies challenge: thru the Smokies in four days. It requires about 19 miles a day minimum and it's some of the

In the Smokies on the NC / TN line

toughest elevation gain yet on the trail. I'm looking forward to hitting the southern boundary tomorrow after dropping my registration off at the visitor's center. Supposed to be a nice day and I'm looking to hit the trail early.

    I got my first bear on camera, the third I've

seen so far. It wasn't ten seconds after I entered the Smokies, I came around the first bend in the trail and he was sitting there watching me, about 30 yards away. He didn't run but eventually walked off down into the woods to search for food and paid me no mind. I've heard this is how the black bears are in the park. They aren't afraid of humans and there are two per square mile in the Smokies, the highest population of black bears anywhere in North America.

Day 12

Location: Silers Bald Shelter

AT Mile: 194.3

Miles Hiked Today: 28.5

The Great Smoky Mountains are fantastic. The most scenic hiking I've had thus far. The climb out of Fontana to get up in the Smokies has been called many four letter words and easy isn't one of them. I was the first out of the shelter this morning and made the climb in the morning while it was still cold out.

The environment here is completely different than GA. It's much cooler. I'm at much higher elevations. There are so many different kinds of trees. Way more views and way more hiking along exposed ridges.

Last night I met a few thru hikers. Lover Boy, who met a girl by Neels Gap and their relationship blossomed into a short-lived trail romance before she had to get off the trail. I've heard of trail romances before, but by Neels Gap? That's the first stop on trail. It has to be some kind of record. Also met Jane and Tarzan. They both ran the Boston marathon before starting their thru. Jane's real name is actually Jane but Tarzan has long hair so his trail name came naturally.

I met two old women and an old man out for a day hike that talked to me for a while today. The man gave me cranberry cookies after hearing I was a thru hiker and I ate them immediately.

At the shelter I was planning on staying at there was a college geology class from Iowa. They had finished exams and had come to the AT to study the rock structures here for a few days with their professor. They were spending the night there and couldn't believe I am doing the whole trail. One girl asked if I carried all the food I would need for months and months. After dinner a couple of thru hikers rolled in that I had passed earlier and were heading to the next shelter north. I decided to join them since dinner had given me more energy. I ended up doing over 27 miles today. I haven't done that much yet and most of the thrus I have met are doing 15 per day tops, so I guess I'm starting to get my trail legs.

Our shelter here is packed and we have a fire going. There's actually a fireplace inside the shelter that's made of stone and has a chimney. I'm welcoming it tonight because it's going to be down in the 30's.

Tomorrow I hit Clingman's Dome, the highest point on the AT at 6,643 ft. I also will cross the 200 mile mark. I'll also hit Newfound Gap, one of the largest road pull offs on the whole trail. It's notorious for being easy to hitch into Gatlinburg from Newfound Gap. It's a significant location for me, because at the gap there should be a plastic bottle stashed under a park structure by my college roommates Tim and Zach. They left it with notes for me to receive during this trip back in January when we spent a weekend up here. I hope it's still there, they tried to hide it really well.

Gatlinburg, TN:

Hitched into Gatlinburg for the night. I didn't expect it to be so hiker friendly. It's so commercialized and touristy but everybody I have interacted with has been so generous. My hitch driver tried to offer me money, my server at Shoney's brought me two Dr. Peppers simultaneously because she saw I was a hiker, the guy at the outfitter filled up my alcohol fuel and didn't charge me a dime, the inn I'm staying in usually charges a rate of $65 a night but for thru hikers it's $29. I can't believe the hospitality I've gotten here.

Day 15

Location: Standing Bear Farm Hostel

AT Mile: 240.8

Miles hiked today: 19

This hostel has been my favorite place on trail so far. Got in today at 2 pm after hiking down from the Smokies in steady rain. Shoes and socks and clothes were soaked. This morning my hands were wet and numb when i started but as I hiked farther I warmed up.

Our shelter last night was over capacity with 16 hikers total. All but two were thru hikers. We made a fire and a big burly man with a mustache named Camel, who is also an ex marine about my father's age, told us stories from his childhood as the flames warmed our chilled legs and feet. He sat with his stumpy feet out by the fire, and I couldn't help but imagine him as a hobbit. Most of the older hikers passed around a bottle of Crown Royal by the fire until it grew dark and we all crawled into our cold sleeping bags.

This is the first real hostel I've stayed at and I love it. It's very rustic and authentic. Curtis, the owner, bought a farm and converted the buildings into a hostel. It reminds me of something out of a civil war picture book. Giant, old AT maps hang in the bunkhouse on the walls. This truly is a hiker hostel. Everything is on the honor system here; you get an envelope, write your trail name on it, then tally up everything you get. I resupplied from a shed where they keep all their hiker food. I was soaked when I first arrived so I got a hot shower, put my wet clothes in the dryer and made a frozen pizza in their pizza oven. I sat in the shack with the kitchen appliances eating as Freebird played on the radio. They have everything from hamburgers to bacon and eggs and you just cook it yourself and tally it up. They sell PBR's straight out of the fridge.

I met the first other ultralight hiker I've seen today. We hiked down from the Smokies together. His name was Bryan and he is trying to do the trail before returning to college in August so he is doing insanely high-mile days regularly. Like 25's every day. He's actually the first person to catch me, he started about three days after I did.

I finished the Smokies in four days which was my goal and still took half a day and a night in Gatlinburg. The first half of the Smokies I had great weather but the second half was nothing but thick fog and rain. The high elevations there do crazy things to the weather. It was usually a black cloud right over me most of the time but on the horizon it would be clear. Frustrating.

I love this hostel so much I think I might come back here when I'm done one day. All of the old wooden porches have swings and there's a creek that runs under the cabin and across a footbridge. The older hiker Camel told us he injured his leg coming down from the Smokies just before reaching Standing Bear two years ago while attempting a thru hike and ended up staying at this hostel for over four months. He liked it so much he just didn't leave.

Going under I-40 today was pretty neat. I hated commuting to work on that thing in NC and it's nice to hike under it and not get stuck in a traffic jam. A lot of hikers are talking about shuttling up to Trail Days, the hiker festival, in Damascus next weekend. I really want to go and me and another thru hiker named Coozy were discussing how we could do it from Erwin, possibly if we make it there by Friday. Hope this rain clears up soon.

Day 16

Location: Walnut Mountain Shelter

AT Mile: 260.8

Miles Hiked Today: 20

Paused on top of Max Patch… I planned my day out so I could have lunch there. It's one of the most renowned balds on the entire trail. Unfortunately my panoramic view consisted of dense clouds of white. Everywhere. I had to wear my shell jacket because it started to rain. Eventually I packed up and moved on. So much for lunch.

I was the first one out of the hostel this morning. I hiked alone for most of the day but talked to quite a few day hikers on top of Max

Patch. They were surprised to hear I was 260 miles into my trip. When I had done 19 miles, just one mile before my shelter, it started to pour. I had to climb the last mile to finish so I decided to leave the rain gear off. When you climb in rain gear it traps your heat and causes you to sweat inside your jacket. The end result was being soaked when I reached the shelter.

There are three of us here tonight. Coozy that I met from last night at Standing Bear and another older hiker that started a month before me but had to take a few weeks off in GA due to a foot injury. The elderly hiker did over 1,200 miles of the trail one summer between school when he was 15! We talked a lot about how the trail has changed. He is using his camera to recreate shots he took when he was a just a kid on the trail.

The shelter here is OLD. It was built in 1938. Holes are everywhere in between the logs and we've already seen a few mice scampering about. We're right on a ridge so if we get rough winds tonight we could be in for a loud night.

This shelter is also apparently known for bear activity. Coozy and I have two different guidebooks and both say something about bears here. His reads, "Bears at this location show no fear of hikers. Use cables…" That's exactly what you want to hear before bed.

Excited about hitting Hot Springs tomorrow. It's a true trail town. The trail actually joins the main street and follows it through town. I'm actually going to post this tomorrow because I have no service here. That seems to be a growing problem that I didn't have the first two weeks.

Day 17

Location: Elmer's Sunnybank Inn, Hot Springs

AT Mile: 273.9

Miles Hiked Today: 13.1

Each hostel I stay in keeps getting better than the last. This hiker inn in Hot Springs will be my home for the night and it's basically a historical monument, an antique on a Victorian scale. The home is over 170 years old. It's one of the most famous inns for thru hikers on the entire trail. They serve handmade vegetarian meals made from their own organic garden and hikers can sign up for breakfast or dinner. The parlor is full of musical instruments; guitars, a banjo, harmonicas, violins…

Mice chewed a hole in my Western Mountaineering down bag last night while I was sleeping in the shelter! I was not a happy hiker this morning when I woke to find pieces of down lying around and a quarter-sized hole in my expensive sleeping bag. I tried to patch it when I got to the hostel. I've never heard of this happening before and neither had any of the hikers I've talked to. Pretty bummed about this all day. I saved up and spent almost $300 on this bag.

Today was a muddy descent down to Hot Springs. 5th day in a row my shoes have been wet. So much rain and low lying clouds in the last few days. The trail comes right off a mountain and onto the main street of Hot Springs. I checked into the Sunnybank Inn around 1 pm. Got lunch at the Smoky Mountain Diner across the street that reminds me of some of the country restaurants back home. I got the salisbury steak, mashed potatoes, green beans and corn bread special with a sweet tea for $5.99. Did my laundry at the laundromat down the street and took a shower at the inn. I bought another bandana at the outfitter because my last one was burned by my stove. Somebody was concerned about my alcohol stove in the Smokies and tried to turn it off when I had turned around, except you can't turn alcohol stoves off, so they ended up burning my bandana. After food I sat out front of the restaurant in the shade eating ice cream as my clothes dried.

This inn is so perfect. I had a glass of wine with thru hiker Ulysses on the back porch. He is from Toronto and has a large manly red beard. He's about my age. Mine is growing but I doubt it will be that big by the end of my hike.

I resupplied at the Dollar General down the street. My next stop will be Erwin TN, about 70 miles from here. Hoping to be there by Friday. My uncle Gary might be coming to meet me for a day, so I probably will push on tomorrow and not take a zero in Hot Springs, although it would be a perfect place to do it. Apparently 30% of the town's population are former thru hikers.

I want to come back here one day to spend a night and revisit Max Patch since it had zero visibility when I summited yesterday. I hope my shoes dry out tonight. Wet socks contribute to blisters. I almost felt a few coming on this morning on the way down. I might have to break out the duct tape to help cover them next time. Hot Springs is the place!

Day 18

Location: Jerry Cabin Shelter

AT Mile: 300.3

Miles Hiked Today: 26.4

Left hot springs around 8:30 this morning after having my second meal at the diner across the street. Had an omelet, grits, toast and a pancake. I crossed the French Broad river and started climbing away from the town. I saw two black tail deer early on and I froze just as they looked my way. We stayed like that for a few minutes: me not moving at all and the deer staring dead at me. I knew as soon as I reached for my camera they would dart and they did.

Ulysses decided to take a zero in Hot Springs today. It was tempting to join. I had to force myself out of that soft warm bed this morning. Had a great night's sleep. I may take a zero in Erwin so maybe he will catch up to me there. He hikes pretty fast.

We have seven people in the shelter recommended for six tonight. I offered to tent out because I haven't in a while but everybody made room for me after I arrived. The Firescald ridge was the highlight of today. Tough rock scrambles but surrounded by pink flowers. I'm not sure what's going on with my service tonight because it shows I have it but I can't make calls. 3G is going in and out so I might have to try and post this tomorrow.

Day 19

Location: Bald Mountain Shelter

AT Mile: 325.1

Miles Hiked Today: 24.8

It's 7:28 pm and I'm already in my sleeping bag. Nobody else at the shelter. Didn't see anybody for the last 15 miles today. Raining so hard now I can barely hear myself think from the pounding on the tin roof. Hope Coozy makes it in but I bet he pulled up short. There was an exposed bald (" properly named "Big Bald") just before this shelter

Crossing a fence stile

and I wouldn't want to cross it in a storm, so I doubt anybody will be joining me tonight.

    I did get a good amount of trail magic today though. First I came upon this mountain top where an old man is sitting by some tombstones and another is mowing the area. I stop to talk and he offered me chocolate. He then asked if I had eaten breakfast and I replied yes but he offered me a ham and cheese sandwich from his cooler and I ate it.

About four miles farther I come across two men with tools heading to work on the last shelter. They offered me soda which I was surprised to find cold. Was feeling pretty good after these two encounters.

One mile before my shelter I cross Big Bald. Panoramic views and I ate what seemed like a pound of peach rings gummy candy while sitting in the sun on top. Kept hearing loud thunder off to the east so I moved on to the shelter.

Made rice for dinner and ate it while reading the shelter log alone here. Started raining just as I hung my food. Tomorrow I have 16.5 miles into Erwin, TN where my uncles Gary and Woody are both coming to see me and have dinner. They live about three hours from this section of trail. I think I will take a zero day in Erwin Saturday, meaning a day of rest and no hiking. I haven't taken one yet. They have a movie theatre and I might try and catch something there. I've been out of the loop for long enough now I don't even know what is playing. Hope the storms hold off later tonight. Maybe I can get some rest.

Thoughts after a few weeks in:

They say wanting to thru hike is a lot like wanting to become an author. Many people want to become writers but not many people want to write. Well many people want to be thru hikers but not many people want to hike. Many come to the AT and realize it's not what they expected. They have an unrealistic romanticized idea of what it's going to be like. They come looking for something, or trying to find themselves... Truth is, there's nothing out here but rocks and trees and mud and roots.

Still, if you look close enough, there is something else. There's friendship, a challenge, an experience, and an adventure like non I've had before.

Day 20

Location: Erwin, TN

AT Mile: about 341

Miles hiked today: about 16

I'm sitting out by the fire at the hostel in Erwin and don't have my guidebook handy so excuse me for not having the exact mileage for today. Nobody else made it into the shelter last night and cold winds blew directly in for most of the night.

I took a picture of the Nolichucky river on the descent down just before Erwin. My uncles Gary and Woody were there waiting for me when I got to the crossing. I checked into the hostel here and got a private cabin so I can sleep in tomorrow.

We got lunch at a country diner and I resupplied. Feels good to be back in town. The strap on my right trekking pole came loose but we got it fixed with a new screw.

After family left I got a shower. One of the thru hikers here named Shelter Stew had a fire going outside the cabins and I stayed around the fire for a while just in my towel drying off. He has a dog hiking with him and has been on trail since February. They are just relaxing most days, never doing more than five miles. He made some blackberry pie tonight and offered me and two other thru hikers some. We put vanilla ice cream on it and sat on the picnic table and ate it under the stars.

I'm thinking about getting a harmonica to carry with me. I think it could be fun to learn out here. A lot of hikers carry backpacking guitars but those seem so cumbersome. Plus I want to learn a new instrument. Mom and dad are coming to see me next weekend. Should be in Damascus, VA by then…

Pretty excited about getting a great night's sleep tonight. No shelter snoring from other hikers! No mice! No inflatable pad on shelter boards!

Still not completely sure if I will zero tomorrow but I doubt I'll do many miles if I don't.

Day: 21

Location: Curley Maple Gap Shelter

AT Mile: 346.2

Miles Hiked Today: 4.7

      Spent most of the day in town in Erwin but decided to push on up the trail to the next shelter instead of taking a full zero and spending another night in town. Bumped into ultralight Bryan at the hostel this morning. Haven't seen him since the Smokies. He had been feeling sick and decided to slow down for a few days. We got a shuttle ride to an all you can eat pizza place for lunch. A lot like Cici's back home… and we both ate so much. Hitched back to the hostel where I took a nap before heading back on trail.

      It was less than 4 miles to the next shelter so I only had to hike for about an hour and a half. Still it was a climb and my pack feels so much heavier loaded down with food and fuel. I was the first one at the shelter but Bryan rolled in right after me, he's now going by the trail name Mercury. No Name and Two Step, a young couple who are engaged, showed up right after us. They are hiking with two dogs, Tess and Molly. You can see Tess by the fire in the picture. It's nice having dogs around camp.

      I made a fire while everyone else unpacked. No Name says they are making cheesecake for us all out of powdered milk and pre made crust.

Mercury in the Roan Highlands

Sounds questionable but maybe it will taste delicious out here.

The shelter here is awesome. It seems the more people the guidebook claims the shelter sleeps, the nicer it is. Maybe this is due to the recent spike in the trail's popularity. So when building new shelters, they tend to make them larger to accommodate the larger number of hikers. Usually when the book says a shelter only sleeps 5 or 6 it ends up being pretty old (read: drafty, mice infested, cramped). The sign here says this one was built in 2010. It's two story and sleeps 14.

So today is my three week mark. I'm still feeling strong. Looking forward to reaching Virginia and seeing mom and dad for the first time on trail.

Day 22

Location: Clyde Smith Shelter

AT Mile: 368.2

Miles Hiked Today: 22

    I stopped for a photo today at a place my guidebook calls the "The Beauty Spot", a small grassy bald that I had read about long before starting my trip. I passed a photographer who looked like he had a giant telescope for a camera and he had it out right on the trail. I asked him what he was shooting and he said birds. The weather today was fantastic and a soft cool breeze blew for most of the afternoon.

    Tomorrow I will climb back over 6,000 ft just before Carver's Gap, a place where Dad and I did a thirteen mile trip north on the AT. So thirteen of the 20+ miles I plan on doing tomorrow I've done before. I'm still looking forward to it because it's one of the most scenic sections of the whole trail. Somebody at the last hostel told me that National Geographic just named it one of the most beautiful AT hikes. This will be the last time I do a section I've done before. I might actually tent out in the same flats I stayed at with dad. Everything north of tomorrow is new to me.

For some reason I was craving a Yoo-hoo today but no trail magic came my way. I might try and dip into Elk Park to grab one on Tuesday.

Day: 23

Location: Doll Flats

AT Mile: 388.9

Miles hiked today: something like 20

Headed out with Mercury today to tackle the Roan Highlands. We had a strenuous hike up to Roan High Knob. Weather stayed nice and we talked about books we had both read and wanted to read again. It dawned on me then that this is the time of year when I usually read, in summer. I don't usually read for pleasure in school. I'm thinking about picking up a light book to carry with me but I'm so tired by the end of most days that I think it would be hard to focus. I've tried reading in some hostels but it puts me right to sleep.

The balds today were awesome and we spent most of the time above tree line. Even doing it for the second time was amazing. If you live in NC or TN and want to hike a gorgeous section of the AT, do Carver's Gap to US 19 E (in that direction, the other way has you climbing about 3,000 feet).

Made it down to Doll Flats where Dad and I

stayed at about a year ago. Ironically this is the first time I've tented out since Franklin and there is thunder and dark clouds looming in the background. Really hoping those don't move this way. Three older guys and two other thru hikers are staying at the flats tonight and the older guys are cooking pizzas over the fire. They offered to share some of their food with us.

I'm almost out of food so looking to resupply in Elk Park or Roan Mountain tomorrow morning. Gary's deer jerky he gave me has come in handy. We're only three miles from the road crossing to resupply, so we might try to get some breakfast somewhere in town too. Not planning on staying long because I still want to try and do 22 miles to another shelter. I will also be searching for my much-longed-for Yoo-hoo.

Day 25

Location: Vanderventer Shelter

AT Mile: 434

Miles Hiked Today: 23.7

I took a photo of the sun out with some incredibly puffy clouds by the shelter this evening but don't let it fool you. It was raining all day and most of yesterday. It just cleared up as soon as we made it in.

I typed up a long entry last night but ended up deleting it by accident when I was trying to post it, so we will jump from day 23 to day 25. I did make it into Roan Mountain (the town) yesterday morning to resupply. Got breakfast at a greasy spoon called Bob's Dairyland. Three eggs scrambled, sausage, a side of bacon, hash browns, four pieces of toast with jelly, a pancake, and a giant cup of blueberry ice cream. A breakfast to remember.

Rained hard today and everything got soaked. Hiked most of the day with Mercury. Another couple named me Quicksilver so I guess that's what I'm going with for a trail name for now. It feels great to have passed the 400 mile mark but getting to 500 sounds even better. I might just hit VA tomorrow and do a 30+ mile day down to Damascus then take a zero Friday. It's smooth sailing for the most part into town from here, elevation hovered around 3,900 feet all day. A few very small climbs. My mom and dad are coming to see me Friday and I can't wait to see them. I miss them a lot.

The last two nights the shelter has been overcapacity. It's literally elbow to elbow. People that arrive late are forced to tent out. I can't wait to stay at "The Place" in Damascus, a hostel that has been famous on the AT for quite a while. It's donation based and operated by the Methodist church. A suggested donation of $5 is all that's required to use their bunk room and facilities.

I'm having the experience of a lifetime out here and every day has brought new challenges and memorable moments. The people I've met have been great and I have been having loads of fun even while "simply enduring" (how one former thru hiker described most of the time out of a given day while attempting a thru).

Excited for Damascus and mom and dad and more ice cream…

CHAPTER 3: THE MID ATLANTIC

Hostel sign at "The Place" in Damascus

Day 26

Location: Damascus, VA

AT Mile: 467.1

Miles Hiked Today: about 33

    Hit the VA border today! So long TN… Hiked with a guy named Leif and his dog Koda today. Leif is a raft guide from Colorado and we talked about all the things we still want to do even after our hikes. There's so many places I want to see out west.

It was fun to hike with a dog for the first time. They stopped at the last shelter before Damascus and Mercury and I pushed down for the last ten miles to make it a 33 mile day. My feet were in the worst pain of the whole trip to date in the last six miles. No blisters, just plantar fascia related. We made it into town and went straight to Quincey's Pizza. There was a bar and people were singing Karaoke. I got a 12" pizza, ate it all, then had 2 scoops of strawberry ice cream.

Made our way over to "The Place" (hostel) and registered for a bunk. Unfortunately there aren't beds here, just wooden bunks, so I'm sleeping on my Neoair again tonight. Got an amazing shower though. My showers end up being ten times longer than usual because it feels like it takes that long to get half as clean as sociably acceptable. At least when you haven't showered in four days. I haven't done laundry since Hot Springs and didn't get to tonight (laundry services are not working here at the moment so I'll have to do it at the hostel next door in the morning) so that means I had to put back on my smelly hiker clothes to sleep in.

Mom and Dad will be here in the morning and they're bringing Dad's new puppy. Looking forward to a relaxing day of zero miles to hike.

Day 27

Location: Damascus, VA

Miles Hiked Today: Zero!

My uncle Gary sent me a brand new harmonica like I've wanted to pick up. I hope I can learn something or two while I'm out here. I woke up early today in The Place and went next door to The Hiker's Inn to do laundry.

Mom and Dad made it up today and we went out to eat at Quincy's Pizza and then went by the outfitter and store to resupply. We went down by the river and I cooled my swollen feet off in the water while the puppy jumped in. We got ice cream at a stand and I ended up trading my blueberry cheesecake for Dad's strawberry.

I wish I could have stayed with them longer but they had to get back and I have more miles to do tomorrow. My feet and toes really needed this zero though. I'm still fairly sore from the big day yesterday.

I'm staying at The Hiker's Inn tonight and the bunk room here is awesome. Air conditioned and mattresses! Seriously though it's basically a brand new house. The caretakers here provide everything you could possibly need too: towels and toiletries and even drinks and snacks. This morning at The Place I ended up drying off from my shower with paper towels from the kitchen. An ultralight hiker would never carry a pack towel though…

It has been a fun time in Damascus. Ready to hit the trail again tomorrow.

Day 28

Location: Whitetop Mountain

AT Mile: 488.2

Miles Hiked Today: 21.1

Last night I met the infamous Old English from England. I had heard his name many times from people he had passed along the trail. We shared the hostel with two other hikers last night: Chop Chop and Patagonia. Old English is a retired school principal and was leaving for home today because his sister was sick. I told him how I wanted to hike the John Muir Trail through the Sierras one day and it turns out he thru'd it last summer. He showed me so many fantastic photos on his camera from the trip.

The AT followed the Virginia Creeper trail for a few miles today - a bike trail that truly is the laziest bike trail on Earth. They shuttle you 15 miles to the top and you coast down. No work required. The trail was wide and families and tourists zipped past me on bikes. They all looked at me like they didn't know why I was out there without a bike. Especially hiking uphill.

I passed a church group from High Point with probably 20 kids of all ages. I played 21 questions with them for a while. You're hiking alone? The whole trail? Do you have a gun? Do you carry all your food for the whole trip? Have you been attacked by animals?

When I hit the bald near buzzard rock there were three hikers there. I had a crazy experience with one… Fifty Plus, who turns out is from Raleigh and the NC State area. We lived about five blocks from each other. He is also friends with my friend Brian from UNC. Also, the other couple, who were section hiking south, we're from Carrboro… So it didn't take us long to realize we were all from the same area and just wound up on this rock in Virginia together. Pretty wild. I could have probably counted the hikers I've met from NC on one hand before this, then I meet three on the same rock in separate parties.

Fifty Plus and I tented out and I made some dinner. I walked up on the ridge above my tent to watch the sunset and took photos in the pink light of dusk. A deer came into our camp and I got a shot of it silhouetted against the fading sky as it was leaving.

I did an estimate: it's going to take me roughly 25 days to do Virginia. It's the longest state on the entire trail and many people get what's called the "Virginia Blues" where the trail starts to wear on them mentally. Hopefully I can stay strong.

Wild ponies

Day 29

Location: Hurricane Mountain Shelter

AT Mile: 510.9

Miles Hiked Today: 22.7

Spirits were high today and I'm not sure if it was the perfect weather, the wild ponies by the trail, or perhaps passing the 500 mile point. Probably a combination of all three. I also passed through the Grayson Highlands State Park which was incredible. Spent a lot of the day above tree line and took in views that stopped me in my tracks. The sun was blazing all day though, and it had drained me by the time I hit the shelter. I had to drink a lot of water once stopped to rehydrate.

I bet I saw over 250 hikers on the AT today, I kid you not. The park here is very popular for its views. Being Memorial Day weekend it seemed that everybody in Virginia decided to come hike the AT. Tons of day hiking families and overnight church groups. It almost felt like I was in an Appalachian Trail city. I stopped for lunch at a shelter and a man with his five kids there was interested in my thru hike. The kids couldn't believe I have been out here for a month (Actually tomorrow marks exactly one month).

Last night around 10:30 pm, right after everybody had crawled into their tents, we heard what I assume was a bobcat screech. I had read about them before but if you had no idea what they sound like it's easy to get unnerved. It's essentially the sound of a woman screaming in the middle of the darkness. We heard it twice and one of the section hikers not far from me started to audibly freak out. Some of the other hikers had heard it before though and assured him everything was fine.

Tonight I'm staying with Waterboy who is 22 and from Atlanta. Really smart and interesting fellow. We're both trying to make it to Partnership shelter tomorrow night which was rated one of the top ten shelters to stay in on the AT. It has showers and is near a road so you can call and order pizza and they deliver. Talk about roughing it… Almost 25% of the way to Maine!

Day 30

Location: Partnership Shelter

AT Mile: 530.6

Miles Hiked Today: 19.7

Ran into a big mama bear and her cub this morning. I startled them and they ran up into the woods. Baby bear decided to climb a tree about 30 yards from the trail so the mom stopped at the trunk and wouldn't budge. I was in a staring contest with her for about 10 minutes trying to decide what to do. I had to get closer to them to get around them and the mountain was too steep to get off the trail. She watched me closely through the trees until I got the courage to slip by them on the AT. Normally bears don't enter my mind but being that close to a defensive mother made me nervous.

Afterward I ran into an overnight hiker who was decked out in military gear. Helmet, ammunition sling, the whole 9 yards. He was hiking to Trimpi Shelter for the night, a shelter erected in memory of a Vietnam casualty. Turns out he was a veteran and I thanked him for his service. He was doing this in honor of memorial day. He told me where his truck was and that magic was in the back in a cooler. I got a delicious ice-cold orange, a soda and a peach-flavored water.

I got a hitch into town by E-How, a driver who was picking up a day hiker I had passed earlier. He took me to the Wal Mart, then to the local diner. We said goodbye and he left to pick up his hiker who's name was Lead Foot. Soon after they both returned, had dinner with me then paid for my food! They even gave me a ride back to the trail... They both are from New Hampshire and Led Foot is day hiking her way until she's done the entire trail. She only has about 390 miles left to do! Can't believe how nice they both were, some of the most generous people I've met on the trail.

What an amazing day. Every day keeps bringing new encouraging experiences.

Three typical trail markings on one sign

Day 31

Location: Knot Maul Branch Shelter

AT Mile: 556.1

Miles Hiked Today: 25.5

Today was hot. I was sweating pretty good by 8:30 am. Much of the day was spent hiking through farmland and fields and pastures, all exposed to the sun. I crossed I-81 near Atkins, VA and there was a local hometown restaurant called The Barn that advertised a 16 ounce hiker burger. I went in and the only other customers there were three thru hikers so I ended up sitting with them. Decided to get chopped BBQ, mashed potatoes, green beans and cornbread instead of the hiker burger.

Dark clouds rolled in around 4 pm and two miles before I hit the shelter it started raining. I actually welcomed it because it was so warm today. The glass has to always be half full on the AT. If it's raining: good, the springs aren't dry. If it's sunny: good, I don't have to hike through muddy trail.

Our shelter is packed with thru hikers and all of our stuff is spread out and mixed up inside the shelter as we try to dry it out from the rain. I made chicken fried rice on my alcohol stove for dinner.

No sign of Mercury, he must be a day or two in front of me. He's moving fast enough I might not catch him again. Still, most of the hikers I meet are surprised to hear I started on April 28th. For example, the thru hikers here tonight all started in March. Oger, Mac, Tree Piper and Candy Man.

Not much of an awning on this shelter and rain has been blowing in every now and then. Some of the rivers I came near today were tempting me to jump in because it was so hot. I'm definitely doing it soon. I've heard of some great swimming holes and even a few popular cliff diving spots farther north.

Can't decide if I want to dip into Bland or Pearisburg or both. There's a Dairy Queen in Bland. Ice cream and showers and drinks with ice in them. Things dreams are made of.

Day 32

Location: Bland, VA

AT Mile: 586.9

Miles Hiked Today: 30 or so

Today was rough. Looked at the guidebook last night and saw an upcoming stretch ten miles long with no water, so I made plans to water up at the last source before it. I show up to the source with about half a liter left and nothing is there. I hiked on, knowing what was going to happen. A few miles into the stretch I went dry. To make matters worse the trail was tough, winding and overgrown over a ridge. Uneven rocks covered the trail and slowed me down, forcing my ankles in directions that were painful. Just as I thought I couldn't get any more parched, I came to a road crossing with multiple gallon jugs full of water and a freshly cut watermelon. It had been left by a trail angel. Nobody was there but I dug right in. The water truly saved me.

I think I've learned one thing about my feet. They don't take kindly to 28+ mile days. If I keep it under 28 they will be sore but anything over and they will start talking to me during the last few miles.

I made it a long day to reach the small town of Bland. I tried to hitch for a few minutes until a lady in a pickup came from the opposite direction to drop off hikers. She asked me if I wanted a ride into town and I replied "Yes mam'." She took me to the Subway restaurant and waited as I ordered food. Then she took me down the road to a dairy queen. I thanked her and ate my sub in the parking lot. Followed that with a banana milkshake and then headed across the street and checked in a motel. Took what felt like the longest and most overdue shower of my life. No shampoo so I washed my hair multiple times with the tiny bar of motel soap as best as I could. Also, the feet. They really needed it.

Now I'm back at the Dairy Queen for seconds. I've been drinking water and just bought a Gatorade but can't seem to quench my thirst. There's so many different kinds of food and drink I want to consume but I know I can't have it all… Tomorrow it's back on the trail.

Day 33

Location: Wapiti Shelter

AT Mile: 613.2

Miles Hiked Today: 26.3

Got up this morning and walked to Subway again for breakfast. Picked up a travel-sized tube of toothpaste from Dollar General and started trying to hitch back to the AT by 9 am. Took me almost an hour to get a ride. I had actually given up and started walking up the mountain when a young local guy offered me a ride.

Today there were no fields or scenic farmland. Just a long green tunnel. Virginia is known as being one of the most mentally challenging states on the trail. In Georgia people quit because they didn't do their research or realize the trail is too tough or for another similar reason. By Virginia, thru hikers quit for different reasons. These are people who have physically proven they can do the whole trail. Still, long hot days of seeing nothing but trees takes its toll. There are over 500 miles of trail in Virginia and much of the terrain is the same. It's the longest state on the AT.

Encountered an incredible remote suspension bridge today. I didn't make it to the shelter until after 7 pm because of my late start and I just knew it would be full of hikers. A storm was brewing behind me as I hiked the last few miles and I didn't want to have to set up my tarp in the rain. Amazingly, even though there were about ten people at the shelter, only one other was sleeping in it. Everyone else is tarped or hammocked out. It ended up being only me and another section hiker in the eight person shelter.

There's another Dairy Queen I have my sights set on in Pearisburg tomorrow. The trail skirts the town so there's not even a need to try and hitchhike in. My kind of trail town.

Oh, also passed mile 600 today.

Day 34

Location: Pearisburg, Virginia

AT Mile: 629.8

Miles Hiked Today: 16.6

I had a cloudy, windy, damp afternoon on my way down to Pearisburg. There were tornado watches in effect for most of the day but luckily I made it into town before the storm really set in. I could see the tiny buildings and houses below me and I had to descend all the way down to them in just a couple of miles, dropping over 2,000 feet in elevation. It was wet and muddy from a small shower that hit in the morning and I actually slipped and fell all the way down at one point while climbing down. I was fine except for some muddy clothes.

I took refuge in a Goodwill when the storm hit.

It was strange being in one again for the first time since starting my hike. Usually I would go every now and then when I was in school or at home. It made me miss going thrifting with my college friends.

    I had to plan where my next stop would be before resupplying at the Food Lion. Logistics on the trail can be a hassle but they can also be fun. I enjoy the planning. I look in my guidebook, determine how many miles it is until the next town i want to resupply in, divide that by how many miles I plan to average per day and there is the number of days of food I need to make it there. In this case it's almost 90 miles to Daleville. If I average 23 miles a day I should have no problem making it in four days so I resupplied with four days of food.

    It's hard not to feel like a homeless person in towns, walking (hobbling) around in clothes that haven't been washed in a week, haven't shaved in a month, smelling like you haven't showered in days, no car, hungry, confused about where you're going… It's no wonder that some people treat you like you're homeless. You can tell that some locals don't like what they call "hiker trash" walking up and down their streets. Still it seems most of the locals are understanding and generous despite our appearance.

    I ran into Yoda today in town, I haven't seen him since Hot Springs, NC. He took a zero today that allowed me to catch up with him. We're both heading north tomorrow so there is a good chance I will be seeing more of him in the near future.

Hiker party at "The Captain's"

Day 35

Location: The Captains!

AT Mile: 650.3

Miles Hiked Today: 20.5

The Captain is a local who lives 30 yards off the trail and he had his annual hiker feed today. Yoda and I hiked together out of Pearisburg this morning to make the feed by 3 pm. It's one of the largest hiker feeds around. We had to ride a short zip line across a stream to reach The Captain's house. They had burgers and hot dogs and fresh fruit and just about every other cookout food imaginable. There's probably 50 hikers here and most people are tented out around the house including myself. Yoda is sleeping under the carport.

They had hiker olympics including limbo, corn hole, statue making out of aluminum foil (one couple made a beer bong which they proceeded to demonstrate during the judging process). It has been a fun day and the 20 miles I hiked earlier flew by. Yoda told me all about his pre AT adventures… He has driven a motorcycle through Alaska and hiked to the Christopher McCandless (Into The Wild) bus, cycled across the country and kayaked most of the Mississippi.

Met quite a few other interesting hikers here. Legs who is a female hiker and about 6'4. Jonah who is hiking with a Siberian husky he rescued eight days before he started. I think I ate more food here than I even do in town. It's nice to hike from sun up til dusk and make miles but I don't feel guilty about doing a 20 and getting to have a little fun and meet more thru hikers. Such a good vibe here and they have music playing and a huge roaring fire going. The Captain is even letting hikers go in his house and use his shower. All of this is free. Once again the kindness from the trail community amazes me. I'm proud to actually consider myself part of it now. I still felt like an outsider at first but after over 600 miles it's hard not to feel part of the trail.

Day 36

Location: Niday Shelter

AT Mile: 680

Miles Hiked Today: 29.7

Hiked all day with Yoda after leaving the Captain's around 8:30. The Captain made pancakes for everybody on the grill. My tent was soaked with condensation. During the middle of the night somebody must have tripped on my guy line on my tent because I woke up with my tent lopsided and almost completely fallen over. I use a trekking pole to pitch it and save weight so it's really not the sturdiest to begin with.

Super tired now from the long day. Many of the climbs today went straight up the mountain and reminded me of Georgia. After I stopped my feet felt like they had been beaten on the bottom with a sledge hammer. Still no blisters or nail problems but they are just really swollen and sensitive. Yoda has serious blisters and skin hanging off his feet in odd places. It's not a pretty sight.

I'm turning in because it's almost 10 pm. I'm

never up this late in a shelter. We got in just before dark. 9:30 pm is hiker midnight… Mile 700 tomorrow!

On the edge of McAffee Knob with storm behind

Day 37

Location: Campbell Shelter

AT Mile: 707.1

Miles Hiked Today: 27.1

Today was pretty brutal but the end was beautiful. Yoda and I had really hard rock scrambles on most of the ridges early on. Some of the rocky climbs were unbelievable. Rebar was used in parts of the rock to serve as handles and steps and resulted in slow going. I ended up cutting the top of my hand on a rock I brushed with the handle of my trekking pole. Also bashed my knee on a ledge trying to pull myself over it. I think it's just a bad bruise but it's still a little swollen and sore.

When we finally made it to McAfee knob it was gorgeous out. We got awesome pics from the rock outcropping and I was actually a little nervous sitting on it since it's so high but I knew I had to do it for the photo. It's one of the most photographed spots on the entire trail and every thru hiker gets their picture taken there. The sunset was just rolling in when we got there. Our shelter was less than a mile past the knob so we didn't mind.

Met Firefox, a girl from Durham and a few other thru hikers at the shelter. We stayed up late in the shelter cooking and talking by headlamp light. Tomorrow I hit the town of Daleville and Yoda has agreed to split a hotel room with me. There's a pool there and a Bojangles down the street! Somebody wrote in the shelter log here "It's Bo Time!" and we all laughed. Amazing day today despite the cuts and bruises…

Day 38

Location: Daleville, VA

AT Mile: 722.5

Miles Hiked Today: 15.4

Climbed over a "fence stile" as listed in my guidebook. I have probably been over close to 25 of these at this point. It requires that you climb a ladder-like structure to get over a farm fence. The first one I came to I thought was really neat, but after a while they aren't as much fun. Usually these are used when crossing cow pastures or other farmland where property boundaries come into play.

Today was not a long day to get to town but it was still punishing. I crossed the Tinker Cliffs and made it into Daleville by around 1 pm. Yoda and I had lunch at the Bojangles then headed for the outfitter. He has never had Bojanges before being from PA. I had to get the tip of my Leki pole fixed that broke back 100 miles ago and has been really annoying to deal with since then. It resulted in me not getting good traction on rocks and was a real safety concern at times. I also spent $21 on a new pair of hiking socks after putting a hole in one of my other three pairs of Smartwool socks. Also got a new bottle of water purification drops because my original supply was about to run out.

Did laundry back at the motel and ended up having to walk down US 220 to a gas station to get $2 in quarters to wash, then back down to another to get quarters to dry since they both had a quarter-request limit. Keep in mind, I'm doing all this while wearing a towel around my waist and a t-shirt. It's interesting being by 220 because it actually goes right by my hometown of Star.

I picked up a very fine print (light) copy of Jack London's "The Call of the Wild" from the Goodwill down the street. It has been a good while since I read it and I've been looking for a book to carry with me. Tonight a thru hiker I met yesterday named Scooby invited me and Yoda over to his room to hang out. We met two other thru hikers from Maine there and we all talked about our aches and pains and different parts of the previous terrain and other hikers we all had met. The longer I'm out here the the stronger my relationships become with other hikers. Some of these I may or may not have even met before. We are all in the same place, experiencing the same weather, the same obstacles, the same trail and we all have the same goal in mind: to thru hike. It's almost like being family. One big trail family.

I will have 1/3 of the trail done by tomorrow night and hopefully will get a full continental breakfast in the morning. Anticipating another good day.

Day 39

Location: Cove Mountain Shelter

AT Mile: 747.5

Miles Hiked Today: About 25

I was on and off the Blue Ridge Parkway so many times today. The trail seemed to follow the road closely and even crossed it five or six times, usually at scenic overlooks and parking areas. I could hear cars and motorcycles for most of the day. At one crossing an elderly couple in a car pulled up and saw me eating my lunch. They found out I was attempting the whole trail and gave me homemade desserts they had stashed in the backseat. I've learned that if I take snack or lunch breaks near road crossings where I could encounter tourists or day hikers I have a chance of getting offered something…

When thru hikers try to get people to give them food or soda without blatantly asking it's called "Yogi-ing". It's taken straight from the cartoon bear in Yellowstone who tries to get people's picnic baskets. I've seen thru hikers start conversations with campers who have big coolers in hopes of them getting something.

I was the first one to leave town today even though I headed out around 9 am. I got a big breakfast in the hotel lobby just before leaving. Bagels and cereal and a waffle. Hiked alone for most of the day and saw lots of deer and my seventh black bear. I was filling a bottle from a spring when I heard something on top of the ridge and saw a bear walking away from me then disappear out of sight.

I am the only one at the shelter here but I think some other hikers might make it this far. There were a few short showers this afternoon so they may have held up at the last shelter.

Really loving this cool weather we've been having lately. I was expecting VA to be hot and it may still be before I'm done. For now it feels good to curl up in my sleeping bag after a long day.

Day 40

Location: Johns Hollow Shelter

AT Mile: 781

Miles Hiked Today: 33 or close to it

This morning I woke to a dense fog and started hiking through it by 7:30 am. Nobody else made it to the shelter last night so I spent the night alone. As I got to the top of the first mountain the sun started to break through and the fog started to disappear. The rays came bright through the mist and I stopped for a photo just before all the fog was completely gone. As I kept climbing I could look down and see a vast ocean of silver clouds before me, with the peaks of other mountains rising above it.

At my first road crossing I met Southpark, a local hiker who had set up a generous trail magic table. I had zucchini bread and brownies and toast and orange punch and he even filled my water bottles for me. I was grateful for the magic because I was about to start a 3,000 ft climb.

Apparently Yoda got in front of me somehow yesterday. It must have been when I stopped at the first shelter just off the trail for a few minutes for lunch. He must have passed me and ended up doing a 30+ mile day thinking I was still in front of him. I saw his name signed in the register and a note about being confused about where I was. I didn't see him today so I think he must have dipped into a town at the last road crossing.

I crossed the James river on the longest footbridge on the Appalachian trail just before my shelter. I had two short thunderstorms this afternoon but now there's just clouds. It rains a LOT on the AT. The higher elevations and the mountains do crazy things to the weather and afternoon thunderstorms are very common. For the past three or four days dark clouds have formed like clockwork around 5 pm. The showers usually don't last long but can still soak you, making for a cold hike into a shelter if winds are blowing hard.

Caught up with Daffy in VA, an old friend

Day 41

Location: Buena Vista, VA

AT Mile: 801.1

Miles hiked today: 20.1

Met up with Sam Ridge, an old hiking friend from Raleigh today in Buena Vista. He is known as Daffy on the trail. I started hiking around 6:45 am and made town by 2 pm. Sam started his thru hike right at the beginning of April but he took some time off and that allowed me to catch up to him. We did a lot of our planning together this past year so it was really cool to see him again.

A day hiker offered me a ride into town immediately after I got off the trail. I went to Hardee's, met up with Sam then we both walked to get ice cream. We hung out in a small wine shop downtown where the owner was being very generous and letting us charge our phones. Got dinner at a Mexican restaurant and then I decided to watch a movie while Sam did some town errands. The theatre here only shows two films and somehow between my choices I ended up seeing What to Expect When You're Expecting. Maybe it was Chris Rock that lured me in but if you haven't seen it yet, save your money.

Sam and I met up again with Yoda at the Burger King. I ate too much too late and felt a little sick. Yoda and I talked about how we passed each other unknowingly twice… That happens when shelters are just off the trail.

Sam and I walked back to the campground on the edge of town and have our sleeping bags and pads laid out under this giant park pavilion with a massive concrete floor where we plan to sleep tonight.

Really tired from today and this inflatable pad sure isn't a bed but I think I will sleep well.

Day 42

Location: Harpers Creek Shelter

AT Mile: 829.3

Miles Hiked Today: 28.2

Incredibly tired. Today felt more like a 35. I actually physically exerted myself to the point of almost passing out today near the end and I've never felt that way before. I was really dizzy for a second and didn't feel well. I watered up, ate a bunch of calories and managed to make it to the next shelter. Calorie crashes happen out here and they pull you down so fast. The problem is you're maybe taking in 4,000 calories of pasta and bread and trail mix throughout the day but you're burning about 6,000. That's why the thru hiker appetite develops.

The soles of my feet felt swollen today, my knees and ankles hurt. It was one of the most physically challenging days I've had. There are two lies on the trail: the first one is that Virginia is flat. It's not as bad as NC or GA or TN but it's far, far from flat. The second lie is that it's only a mile to the next thing you're asking about. We hear that one a lot. It's always more than a mile.

On the bright side I got the most amazing trail magic of the trip today. We crossed a road where four past thru hikers from the 2008 season were grilling and had coolers of soda and fresh fruit. I had a giant orange and grapes and a hot dog and it really hit the spot.

I'm in my sleeping bag and so tired I can barely stay awake so I'm calling this one done.

Day: 43

Location: Waynesboro

AT Mile: 856.5

Miles hiked today: About 27

Finished the day at the start of the Shenandoah National Park. Last night was miserable. It was too warm to really get in my sleeping bag but mosquitos and no-see-ums bit me all night. It was a viscous cycle of getting bit, covering up with the bag, sweating, uncovering, getting bit, repeat.

That's not the only painful insects I've ran into. A few days ago a bee or yellow jacket, I'm not sure which, flew right into my ear while I was hiking. It was stuck there for just a second, the sound was so loud, like an entire hive was in my ear, before stinging me. The ear is a sensitive place to get stung and it swelled up like a balloon and I could feel and hear it pulsing for about an hour afterward.

There's also a plant that stings. It's called Stinging Nettle. I've never heard of it before. It can grow over waist high and has these hollow stinging hairs that literally act like hypodermic needles and inject you with chemicals that produce the stinging sensation. It's like something out of Jumanji. Last night I was stuck by one for the second time this trip while trying to get to a stream to get water. It feels like a bee sting.

The hiking today was too hot for comfort. No breeze at all. My shirt was drenched by 9 am after a 2,000 foot climb. I wrung it out at the top of the mountain and it was as if it came straight out of a swimming pool. I really needed that shower I ended up getting in town later. Yoda and I also checked out the all you can eat Chinese buffet that turned out to be luxurious, or maybe it just appeared that way to two ravaged hikers. They had all the strawberry ice cream we could eat.

I haven't taken any ibuprofen at all on the trail yet but I think that's about to change. My feet have been more swollen than usual lately and I can't tell if it's because my trail runners are finally losing their cushion or if it's just because of the longer days and miles. I'm pretty sure it's both.

Day 44

Zero in Waynesboro

Had originally decided to hike seven miles out of town today but a lot of factors contributed to me taking my second zero of the trip. My feet are still swollen, it rained all day and Yoda and I were still exhausted from doing big miles to get here. Also, mom and dad might come see me in the Shenandoah on Wednesday and I would actually hit the meeting point in stride without having to slow down if I took today off. During my research for this trip I learned that meeting friends and family on trail is always difficult because you never really know exactly where you will be at this time next week or ten days from now, etc. so it makes it hard to plan.

I think I figured out my foot problem. I believe my trail runners are just worn out. Apparently they are only good up to about 500-700 miles then they start to lose their cushion and support, even if they don't look like they're falling to pieces. Mine look fairly well still but I ordered a new pair from the hotel lobby computer to be sent to the post office in Harpers Ferry 150 miles from here. This means I will have put over 1,000 miles on my current shoes by the time I get there. Below the shipping address I added "Please hold for AT thru hiker" and hopefully they will arrive before I do next weekend. Same model, same size, same color. These got me here and I hope the new ones can get me to Maine, or at least close to it.

Tomorrow I head back out on the trail bright and early rain or shine.

Day 45

Location: Pinefield Shelter

AT Mile: 889.5

Miles Hiked Today: 33.2

Wet wet wet. Everybody is trying to dry their

gear and shoes out by the fire. Shelter is packed so I had to tarp out. Rained all day off and on but mostly on. Hardest rain I've had all trip. Everything got soaked: shoes, socks, pack, tent which was inside my pack liner and me, even though I had a rain shell on most of the day. Water finds a way in. There's nothing you can do about it but put your head down and hike.

All day I was hiking in the Shenandoah National Park. It's a popular park and the terrain is much easier than other parts of the trail. I don't think there's a single climb over 1,000 ft and the trail through the park is over 100 miles long. The trail follows closely to Skyline Drive, an extension of the Blue Ridge Parkway. There was actually a general store operated by the park only 75 yards off the trail. I stopped and got a ham and cheese sandwich and a pint of peach ice cream.

When I left the store I started to get bad chafing from being wet all day, especially on my thighs. It was so painful I had to stop quite a few times. I have to try and find something soon to use on it to decrease the friction. My feet looked like prunes when I pried my socks off once I got in camp. I'm meeting mom and dad tomorrow at noon only 11 miles from here so it should be an easy day. I got dad a Father's Day present at the last outfitter that I'm going to give Dad tomorrow. This might be the last time I see them on my trip. Hope tomorrow is dry.

Day 46

Location: Elkton, VA

AT Mile: 901.1

Miles Hiked Today: 11.6

Family day, and I still got to hike this morning. Mom and Dad came up with our neighbors and church friends Benny and Carol Stewart. It was nice to not have to hitch into town. I sat by the side of Skyline drive reading and drying out my tarp and rain gear until they picked me up around 1. We went straight to a Mexican restaurant where i gave dad his father's day present: an AT hat i picked up and carried over 40 miles since the last outfitter in Waynesboro. Afterward, we all hung out in a shady field playing with the puppy while dad sprayed my clothes with permethrin, a chemical that wards off ticks. Deer ticks are more prevalent north of VA and they are known to carry Lyme Disease.

I resupplied at a pharmacy and Food Lion and the Stewarts even paid for my resupply food, so nice of them. We went to Dairy Queen and had ice cream before mom and the Stewarts had to leave. Dad drove separately and stuck around until about 9:30 pm. We went to Subway, got sandwiches and took them to a little league field where we watched an 8 year old softball team practice.

A local church was having a tent revival and we stopped by to ask them if there was somewhere nearby I could pitch my tarp. The motels and campgrounds near the Shenandoah are ridiculously expensive and I didn't want dad to have to pay for a room for just me. The pastor said I could pitch it anywhere. I thanked him and chose a grassy flat spot away from their activities. Later, dad and I sat under the tent watching the revival before he had to leave. I was really glad I got to see them once more and it meant a lot to me that the Stewarts decided to come visit too. Every day now I get farther and farther from home.

Passing the 900 mile mark felt great this morning but all I can think about now is the 1,000. Today is significant for another reason as well; the world record for the fastest Appalachian Trail completion is 46 days held by Jennifer Pharr Davis and was set last season, the same amount of days I've been on trail. Considering it takes many about six months to thru, 46 days is astonishing. Several things were very different about Jennifer's hike though. She ran much of the trail and was also fully assisted. This means she had someone (her husband in her case) follow her in a car and meet her at every road crossing possible to give her water or food or take her to a hotel. This means she didn't have to carry a full pack. Still, it's an amazing accomplishment for her. I'm glad a female holds the record. It shows up some of these other young guys who think they are tough stuff. Tomorrow I continue my trek through the Shenandoah.

Day 47

Location: Birds Nest #3 Hut

AT Mile: 932.5

Miles Hiked Today: about 31

I woke up staring at hundreds of drops of condensation hanging precariously over my head on the inside of my tarp, poised to fall at the slightest brush of the tent wall. All this from being pitched out in the open on the church lawn. Just getting out of my tarp proved difficult because every bump sent drops falling to soak my sleeping bag and gear. The pastor came out and offered me a sausage and egg biscuit that his wife made using eggs from his own chickens. He even gave me a ride back to the trail. I said thank you and headed back into the woods by 7:30 am.

The Shenandoah National Park seems very commercialized in some ways. There's lots of tourists in Winnebagos, restaurants and upscale housing and cottages inside the park. The trail is even trimmed by park employees with weed eaters, leaving the grass next to the trail looking like a front lawn. I found myself being pulled in two directions: in one breath I said to myself that all the commercialism impacts the trail in a negative way, preventing hikers from escaping the world they left for the trail in the first place. Then one hour later, I find myself walking into the Shenandoah Skyland Resort restaurant and bar with the look of a child in a toy store on my face. I can get ice cream right next to the trail?! Fantastic.

The restaurant was very upscale, servers dressed up, all guests in their evening Sunday's best… Then I see four other thru hikers sitting at the bar and I join them and get two scoops of blackberry ice cream. At one point the bartender leaned over to us and sat back quickly with a startled look on his face… Then commented on how we all smelled pretty rough. We all knew he was right.

The shelter I made it to tonight is one of the best I have stayed in. Giant fireplace and a big roaring fire someone started. Sunset from the shelter was stunning and I met many new thru hikers I had never seen before. Tink, a young girl named after Tinkerbell who always wears a ninja turtle toboggan. Also Pops, a tall, skinny, older guy with long hair in braids who speaks with a strong northern accent and has a great sense of humor. He gave me marshmallows to cook over the fire.

I can't wait to get to Harpers Ferry on Sunday. I've had my sights set on it since I left Damascus almost 500 miles ago.

Day: 48

Location: Front Royal, VA

AT Mile: 963.4

Miles Hiked Today: 30.9

Many tents were pitched around the shelter I stayed in last night. This morning was chilly and I could see my breath rise above me while I lay tucked in my sleeping bag. I didn't want to get out but the shelter was already stirring with other hikers so I got up, ate a small breakfast of granola bars, dried fruit and a honey bun then hit the trail.

I met a blind hiker this morning named Trevor Thomas who has thru hiked the AT and the PCT. He was testing gear for some sponsors and is planning to do the Mountains to Sea Trail in NC next. I knew of the trail but wasn't aware it was finished. It winds about 1,000 miles from Clingman's Dome to the coast in NC. Meeting Trevor in person on the trail was an inspiration.

I crossed the northern park boundary around 5 pm. The Shenandoahs were long and green with limited views, not to mention expensive to eat and resupply in. I was ready to put them behind me. As soon as I crossed the boundary I hit a sharp descent of jagged rocks that littered the trail, slowed me and hurt my feet. It was almost comical, as if the park itself were saying "That's what you get for wishing me done."

As soon as I hit the road I got a hitch from a guy on his way to pick up food at an Italian place. I said, "Sounds good to me." I got a pizza and sat in the corner eating by myself. The waitress said to me, "YOU HIKE ALONE? YOU'RE NOT AFRAID OF BEARS?!" I replied "No mam', not unless I'm sleeping with this pizza under my head." I forgot to mention in yesterday's entry that I saw my eighth bear. This one actually did startle me because it must have been asleep beside the trail when I walked up on it. It jumped up at the last second and took off through the woods full speed like a bulldozer, plowing over everything and crashing into trees. Probably the largest bear I've seen yet.

I told myself I wouldn't but I ended up getting the cheapest motel room I could find in town and getting a shower. I still won't be able to wash my clothes until Sunday.

Somebody stopped their car on the road today next to me while I was walking on the sidewalk and said hey, are you a traveler? Do you want some money? Then started reaching for their wallet. I said no thanks, but I couldn't believe somebody would actually stop in the middle of the road and try to give me cash. This trip really has shown me the best side of people that I had never seen before. Moving out early again tomorrow.

Day 49

Location: Sam Moore Shelter

AT Mile: 993.9

Miles Hiked Today: 30.5

Got a hitch out of Front Royal on the back of a truck. Hiking for so long has made vehicles feel so fast. I felt like I was moving at light speed.

I passed a sign today that read "Hikers Beware: Now Entering THE ROLLERCOASTER." My guidebook describes it as 13.5 miles of ascents and descents. You don't need a ticket to get on. It's not that kind of ride. I did almost seven miles of it before reaching my shelter and it was the hardest thing I've done in a while.

Squatch and his friend are staying here with me tonight. They made a fire to boil water because they don't carry stoves. I thought I was going to be spending the night alone again. Out of Virginia tomorrow.

At the Appalachian Trail Conservancy

Day 50

Location: Harpers Ferry, WV

AT Mile: 1017.3 (yeah 1,000!)

Miles Hiked Today: 23.4

    I did the infamous photo-log entry for the AT Conservancy's thru hiker book for this year. I was thru hiker number 528 to sign in at Harpers Ferry. In GA I was number 996 to start from the visitors center, but others probably started directly from Springer mountain or may have never signed in. This means about half of the other starters I either passed or they quit.

    I was up by 5:30 am to get ready to hike. Birds were going nuts so I couldn't sleep anyway. I wanted to get a head start on getting into town too. I made it out of the roller coaster and passed the 1,000 mile mark then entered West Virginia. I crossed the Shenandoah River on a long car bridge and watched the kayakers and swimmers playing below. I took a side trail to the ATC just before town. In my mind I thought the ATC would have been a lot bigger but it was just a small old building with a tiny museum, pictures, information, AT merchandise and a hiker lounge. They did have an old summit sign from Mount Katahdin, the highest mountain in Maine which serves as the northern terminus of the trail.

    Harpers Ferry is such a milestone for thru hikers. I'm staying at The Town Inn and it's right in the middle of the historic district. I can see the Potomac and train tracks that tunnel into the mountain from the balcony. I got a bunk in their Friendship Room, basically a hostel. They do have private rooms but they came with a touristy price tag. Did laundry, took a long shower, they gave me some town clothes to wear around while my clothes washed, got dinner across the street, ice cream, the whole nine yards. Talked to a few tourists who were really interested in my hike. One family gave me question after question in front of the ice cream shop.

Went to the outfitter to see about getting new inserts for my new shoes that are now trapped in the post office until tomorrow morning. The owner there was astonished that I made it this far with one pair of ultralight shoes. He said I was only the 2nd hiker to bring in a pair of shoes this year that I actually hiked all the way here from Georgia in. In other words, I really need new shoes. I decided to wait until tomorrow to get the insoles once I have the new trail runners on.

Being Sunday evening a lot of the tourists were leaving and by sunset I had the whole historical district almost to myself. I walked around looking at the old Civil War landmarks, houses and churches.

Apparently there is a popular German documentary on the AT out in the past year because a record number of German hikers are out this year trying to thru hike. One older couple is sharing the Friendship Room with me tonight. The woman's name is Socks and she went on and on about the documentary… "This film is lies! It doesn't mention blister, or thunderstorm, or mud or…" etc.

Trying to catch a bus to Wal Mart tomorrow before heading out. Don't plan on doing big miles since I'll have the new shoes on. Getting closer to the halfway mark.

Day 51

Location: Crampton Gap Shelter

AT Mile: 1027.7

Miles Hiked Today: 10.4

Really neat shelter that I'm staying in tonight. There's an enormous porch, it's clean inside. I'm in Maryland now. By Wednesday I'll be in Pennsylvania if not by tomorrow. These states will go by so fast compared to Virginia.

Did a short day this evening because I didn't get out of town until around 2 pm. Ran a lot of errands this morning. Took the bus from Harpers Ferry to Wal Mart and resupplied. Also got a cheap foam pad from the camping section that I cut up and made custom-sized strips that I duct taped to the inside of my hip belt to help make it smaller.

On the way back I got dropped off at the post office where I got my new shoes and mailed my old ones home to keep as a sort of souvenir. My new shoes felt like clouds wrapped around my feet. Before I headed out I went back by the outfitter and got new arch inserts to put in my shoes. There was a Jack Russell Terrier there named Duke that was the owner's and I played with him while my trekking poles were worked on. It made me miss Petey, my Jack Russell that we had to put down last summer. I got a cotton candy milkshake before crossing the Potomac on a train bridge then headed back onto the trail.

The woods were wet from the morning rain but not a drop fell before I reached the second shelter. There's a couple here with me tonight that go by Sitcom and Burg. They are doing a 1200 mile section from Damascus back home in Massachusetts. We had good conversation over dinner.

One of the things I like most about the trail are the smells, and I don't mean of other hikers. I'm talking about the plant life and vegetation that grows along beside the trail and the flowers and moss and the fields and the farmland. There are so many different smells that come across the trail and my senses seem heightened after being out here since April. There's a fern in particular that I can always recognize. When I walk near it a sweet, almost syrupy aroma reaches me and I just want to stop and take deep breaths of it.

Thinking about doing a long day tomorrow but I'll see how the weather turns out. Right now a dense fog is coming in. Everybody is saying it's going to be in the 90's by Wednesday and possibly close to 100 degrees. Not ideal hiking weather.

Day 52

Location: Pen Mar Park

AT Mile: 1057.9

Miles Hiked Today: 30.2

I climbed up the "Washington Monument" of

the AT this morning. There was no water for the first seven miles and the spring at the shelter last night was dry so I ended up going without for a while.

I made it to a road crossing near Pen Mar Park that goes into Waynesboro, PA (I'm right on the border, I won't be in PA until tomorrow) and as soon as I started to try and hitch to the Wal Mart to get ice cream a car with three young guys in it picks me up. They are curious about my hike and we end up stopping by their house on the way in where they gave me sodas and ice cream and the conversation kept going. They even gave me a ride back to the trail. Didn't even end up going to Wal Mart. They offered me their couch to sleep on but I told them I was going to try and head out early in the morning. They gave me a ride back to the park here where I'm just sleeping under a park pavilion.

Tomorrow morning I will cross the Mason Dixon line into PA. I've never been this far north before. Can't believe I've made it so far but I still have a long way to go.

Day: 53

Location: Birch Run Shelter

AT Mile: 1086.1

Miles Hiked Today: 28.2

So hot today but it turned out to be one of the best days I've had on trail. Hikes with three other thru hikers about my age: Boots, 3-10, and Hammer. We hit a pool at a state park after about 19 miles into the day. It was perfect timing because the temp was just getting into the 90's and we were soaked in sweat. I showered with my clothes on in the shower house in an attempt to clean them some. The pool felt amazing. I shamelessly stood in line to slide down the children's water slide, twice.

I hung out by the pool from 1 until 3:30. I met an older thru hiker named Plant Man (he's vegan) from New York. His wife was coming to meet him and he asked me if I wanted to go eat with them. We rode in their Prius to a restaurant called the Flamingo and I had lasagna and ice cream. They paid for my food and even gave me their info to get in touch with them once I'm in NY.

They dropped me off at the park and I hiked another nine miles to this shelter. All the shelters since the beginning of Maryland have been ridiculously nice. This one actually has bunks in it. One I passed had a swing out front. At one location there were two small shelters side by side and one read SNORING and the other read NON SNORING.

Unfortunately last night was miserable. Mosquitos ate me alive. I tried covering up with my down bag and it just made me sweat to the point that I was afraid I would get my down soaking wet. The sweating and biting kept me awake all night.

I'm so close to the midpoint on the trail. There's

a unique sign there that I have seen photos of on AT blogs. It's only about four miles away and I'll pass it tomorrow morning. There's also an ice cream place on the trail that is notorious for the half-gallon challenge. I'm hesitant to take it but since I skipped the four state challenge (end of VA through WV, MD, and into PA) I might just accept this one.

So much fun out here today. Going to be hot again tomorrow. If only I had a pool every 20 miles.

Day: 54

Location: Alec Kennedy Shelter

AT Mile: 1111.3

Miles Hiked Today: 25.2

Today was unforgettable for many reasons, first being that I passed the halfway point this morning. It's exciting to think about actually being closer to Katahdin than Springer. I also did the half-gallon ice cream challenge today over lunch and it was a lot easier than I had expected it to be. I felt like my tongue was frostbitten afterwards but getting the full half-gallon down was no problem at all, I almost went back for more.

Had several tough rock scrambles today where I had to actually use my hands, although in general the terrain has been pretty easy lately, at least in terms of elevation change. PA is actually flat in many sections although the northern half is famous for being some of the rockiest sections of the whole trail. Sometimes hiker's feet won't touch soil for days.

Unbelievably HOT today. My shirt was soaked when I rolled into this shelter. Talked to Mom earlier and she said it is actually a little cooler in NC than it has been here. I knew it was going to get hot soon but I didn't expect this heat wave. Springs and streams seem to be staying wet for the most part through it. I believe rain is in the forecast for tomorrow evening.

My plan is to get up early tomorrow and hit it hard before it gets too hot.

The Doyle Hotel in Duncannon

Day 55

Location: Doyle Hotel in Duncannon, PA

AT Mile: 1140.8

Miles Hiked Today: About 30

Most thru hikers, when they complete their journey, create a "thank you" postcard with their summit picture and trail name displayed on it and send copies of it out to all the people and places that helped them along the way. Some get really creative. There was an entire wall of them at this hotel in Duncannon. I look forward to making my own when I finish. There's so many people that have helped me tremendously already.

When i came down from the mountain this morning I emerged into a beautiful and calm cornfield in a valley. It was still very early and the sky was smeared with pastel blues and hints of purple mixed with the warmer light from the sunrise. The first 20 or so miles today flew by. I was in the valley and hiking through lush, flat farmland and was able to make great time. I cruised straight through Boiling Springs (the trail went through the town for a ways) and resisted the urge to dip into a diner for a big greasy breakfast. Other hikers I stayed with at the shelter last night (including TalksALot - she does talk A LOT) were planning on stopping but I had my sights set on Duncannon and the Doyle. I knew if I got there early I would have time to wash my clothes, shower and get a good dinner.

I made it by 3:30 pm despite the last six miles of trail that were completely strewn with sharp rocks. I haven't truly hit the famous PA rocks yet, but I will within the next week. All I've gotten so far is a little taste. I've even heard northern PA called Rocksylvania…

When I strolled into the hotel here the caretaker, Vicky, went straight to work getting everything set for me. Her and her husband Pat own the hotel and they love hikers. They keep logbooks full of pictures of all the thru hikers that come through each year and they took mine as I was mid bite on a burger. The hotel is ancient in American terms, over 100 years old. I love staying at the rustic places. They're so full of history. There's a full service bar and restaurant downstairs and my room is on the third floor. No AC but each room comes equipped with a giant fan. At least I have no biting flies to worry about tonight.

I'm beginning to perfect the art of getting to town with almost no food in my pack. This is important because the weather has been so hot and springs have been so sparse that I've had to carry full water weight up many climbs in the past few days. The last thing I want is another few pounds of unnecessary food that I won't eat before my next resupply being hauled up with me.

A trail angel that stopped me while I was going into a nearby convenience store told me she would give me a ride to the closest grocery store tomorrow morning to resupply. Her name is Trail Angel Mary and she's very famous in the hiking community and has even been featured on an AT documentary. She's essentially an Appalachian Trail celebrity. Getting access to a grocery store is great for the budget because convenience store prices near the trail can sometimes be out of this world.

I really like this town, wouldn't be surprised if I made it back one day...

Day: 56

Location: Campsite

AT Mile: 1157.2

Miles Hiked Today: 16.4

Had to eat dinner inside my tent this evening because the mosquitoes were at it again. I watched six them hovering just outside of my mesh wall trying to get in at me. The dried pepperoni stick and pizza flavored combo snacks went pretty well together. I always lay my headlamp out by my head whether I'm in a shelter or my tent and the guidebook is usually there too where I'm trying to determine where I'll hike to the next day, what the water sources look like, what the terrain will be like, etc.

I'm pitched off the trail and not at a shelter. I chose this campsite because the shelter spacing out of Duncannon was troublesome. I could either do an 11 mile day or a 30 mile day, neither of which I wanted to do. I probably would have went farther but I ran into a young guy named White Wolf at the first shelter where I stopped for water and hiked with him the rest of the way in. He hiked slower than me but I enjoyed the company. We talked about surfing and our experiences in college and the trail. There's no water at our campsite and there wasn't water since the first shelter, so I had less than a liter to use for the evening. PA water sources are known to be few and far between. Luckily it wasn't quite as hot today and there was a small breeze blowing.

I got quite a late start out of Duncannon. Walked to Trail Angel Mary's house down the street around 9 am and found three other hikers sitting in her kitchen debating politics. She had let them stay the night. Eventually she gave us all a ride to the store to resupply. By the time I got back, grabbed some breakfast across the street at Goodie's Diner and packed up all my stuff and organized my food it was almost noon.

The social aspect of the shelter scene is nice but it's also peaceful to just be tented out on top of a ridge away from all the commotion. It's also easier to sleep in a tent than the shelter.

Got sad news from a section hiker in the diner this morning. Greenhorn, a thru hiker I met back in northern Virginia, dropped out at Harpers Ferry. He seemed to be doing great when I met him so I'm not sure what happened. The trail can be a roller coaster of emotions at times. I hope he makes it back one day to finish.

Day 57

Location: 501 Shelter

AT Mile: 1187.6

Miles Hiked Today: 30.4

Was hiking by 6 am today and left White Wolf sleeping in his tent. After about ten miles I ran into a young hiker named Lighthouse. I had seen his name in the shelter logs. He's from Scotland and came to the US just to do the trail. We hiked together for another ten miles before he stopped for a late lunch. I pushed on and did the last ten alone and fast. I made it to the 501 road crossing around 4:45 pm.

It took about 20 minutes to get a hitch. The car dropped me off at an Italian pizza place in Pine Grove, PA. A church youth group there watched amused as I ate a whole medium pizza and drank an entire two liter of Pepsi in about 45 minutes. I've realized that if the trail miles to a town are just right I can often do a big day and still have time to get in for a dinner, get back on the trail, make it to the next shelter and not have to stay in a motel room or hostel in town. This is awesome because I can get calories and carbs and still save money on expensive lodging.

I hitched back to the trail and went to the nearby 501 shelter. It's in a family's backyard that lives near the trail and they serve as caretakers. It actually has four walls and a skylight. It's really more like a guesthouse. No power but it does have an outdoor shower which I used to wash my hair. It feels amazing to use outdoor showers. I wouldn't be opposed to having my own back home to use in the summer.

The thru hikers on the trail at this point are very different from the ones I knew in Georgia. These hikers are seasoned, "green" as one ridge runner told me, meaning we don't trash the environment. They are also determined. You can see it in them. Every person I meet has something in them that drives them not to quit. I don't always notice it right away, but it's always there and usually becomes apparent somehow after getting to know them. It's like the trail has become an essential part of our existence and our lives. It's hard for me to conceive of doing anything other than hiking at this point.

Big milestone today, even more significant to me than reaching 1,000 miles hiked. Today I passed the 1,000 miles *left* to hike mark. I am now down to three digits. Into the 900's. I think from this shelter it is something like 996 miles to go. Still a very, very long distance but when you have had thousands of miles hanging over you for months, it feels great. I feel like I can now start counting DOWN to the end of the trail instead of counting up. I remember reaching the 100 mile point, the farthest I had ever hiked up until then, and thinking "I still have over 2,000 miles to go"… That can be discouraging.

Heading for a Cracker Barrel tomorrow.

Day 58

Location: Hamburg, PA

AT Mile: 1212

Miles hiked today: 24.4

Last night I made the mistake of telling another hiker that I hadn't been caught in a really bad electrical storm yet on trail. I even knocked on wood. This morning changed all that. As soon as I left the shelter it started to rain. Light at first, then harder. I climbed high up on a ridge and the rain continued. Once I was on the very top lightning began flashing everywhere. It was the loudest storm I've ever experienced. It doesn't matter how long you've been in the woods, if you're on top of a mountain in pounding rain and severe lightning it puts your senses on edge. The storm lasted for about an hour.

When it ended I was soaked, shoes sopped in mud up to my ankles and hips beginning to chafe from my pack's hip belt straps. I pressed on over the rocks and mud until I came to the road crossing that went to Hamburg.

This road was an interstate and my first attempts to hitch failed. I took off on foot and walked the 2 miles extra into town. Tractor and trailer trucks flew past me at 80 mph only feet away. I had no room to move over because of the guardrail.

I headed straight for the Cracker Barrel, my

first on trail. It was strange to walk into it after being subject to such harsh conditions on the trail today. People looked at me like they didn't understand why I was carrying hiking poles into the restaurant. This isn't really a "trail town" and I'm sure some people don't even know about the trail here.

I ended up getting a room at the Microtel next door for the night. I guess this is my one splurge for a nice hotel. It has been worth it. Met an older hiker named Bucket in the restaurant / bar downstairs. We dried our clothes together in the dryer. One problem with hiking fast is that I meet all these really nice, interesting, awesome people then I never see them again, ever. I guess that happens in life outside the trail too though.

Tomorrow I start the rockiest section of Pennsylvania. Rocksylvania. Hopeful that the soles of my feet get a good night's rest.

Day 59

Location: Allentown Shelter

AT Mile: 1233.9

Miles Hiked Today: 21.9

Today the weather was incredible. A stark contrast from yesterday. Sunny skies and a strong, cool breeze blew steady all day. I stopped at an overlook for lunch. The warmth of the sun was so comforting I almost decided to take a nap there. Instead I pushed on.

Rocks did get worse today. I boulder hopped for quite a few miles. Saw a milk snake that I thought at first was a copperhead. All the locals I have met and talked to on the trail here say this area is full of snakes. They crawl up on the warm rocks to bathe themselves in the sun.

I finally ran into the infamous hiker Pants On Fire today at the shelter when I got in. I had heard about this thru hiker before from many others that had met him. When it's hot he hikes in a pink skirt. Today however he was wearing normal shorts because the weather was so nice. He is hiking with his girlfriend, Daystar, and I talked with them as I made my dinner. I had four-cheese mashed potatoes with sliced salami that I tossed in with it. Wasn't quite as good as the Cracker Barrel in Hamburg but it is actually not bad.

The breeze and cooler weather kept the insects at bay today. Hoping tomorrow is just as nice.

Rocky trail in Pennsylvania

Day 60

Location: Unmarked Campsite

AT Mile: 1256.2

Miles Hiked Today: 22.3

    Was hiking by 7:30 am and considered it a late start. Never before would I have considered doing anything at 7:30 am a "late start" until I started this trip. The trail today seemed as if the blazes had been painted 20 years ago and those that were visible were sparse. This made it difficult to follow the trail when there's no soil, only rocks. There was no trail at all at times really. I was just trying to hike from blaze to blaze. I spent a good bit of the morning asking myself if I was actually still on the trail. This makes for slow goings and prevents me from doing the 30+ mile days like I was stringing together earlier in Virginia.

The rocks are more of a mental challenge. You have to engineer every step and plan them out two or three steps ahead at times. After I crossed the Lehigh river I started a famous climb known as Dante's Inferno. It's one mile straight up on a rock scramble. Fences were alongside a road below me to prevent falling rock from reaching traffic. I had to use both of my hands for most of the climb. At this point it was no longer hiking, it had essentially become rock climbing. Some rocks were loose and I was glad to be done with it once I reached the top.

One of the aspects about the trail that I enjoy the most is the freedom. I have no schedule. I have nobody telling me to be here or turn this in by this date or to do anything. I don't know what I'll be doing at this time two days from now, a week, a month. I don't even know for sure what U.S. state I'll be in. the trail is mine to explore however I like. I love this flexibility. I can be as whimsical or rigid as I please. If it's hot and I see an awesome swimming hole I can stop early and swim. If there's a great view I can camp nearby and watch the sunset. If I'm tired of backpacking food I can hitch into a town from a road crossing and find a restaurant. These decisions aren't always planned out and that's what I like about them.

Tomorrow I'm hoping to make the Delaware Water Gap. There's a church there that runs a free hostel for hikers. The terrain should determine if I make it or not. This gap is just before the New Jersey state line so it would be nice to know that I'm done with Pennsylvania for good.

Day 61

Location: Delaware Water Gap, Church of the Mountain Hostel

AT Mile: 1287.7

Miles Hiked Today 31.5

The hostel I am staying in tonight is operated by a church and they don't charge hikers for stay. They only accept thru hikers and long-distance section hikers.

Today was a tough 31 mile day. The rocks were just as bad but I was determined to make this hostel. Again water was difficult to find early in the day. I ended up having to hike a mile out of the way just to reach a source. When you're hiking 30+ mile days, just walking a few extra yards out of the way is mentally painstaking because it's not bringing you any closer to your goal.

In the last 4 miles I ran into Mr. Fabulous, a thru hiker that I went on to hike into town with. We talked about the lack of trail magic in the last state, the rocks, food and New York City because that's where he's from. We both plan on being near the city next week and going in for a few days. He has family and I have an old friend from Governor's School who attends NYU and has offered to take me in for a few days. I've actually never been to NYC before. I said I've never been this far north right?

When we got to the hostel I had just enough time to shower before the church began their weekly hiker feed. It's every Thursday during the hiking season. There's hot dogs and anything else church members decided to bring. It was surreal to walk out of the woods and have so much food in front of me. About 25 church members showed up and brought all kinds of dishes and desserts. One even made homemade peach ice cream. There was jello with so much fruit in it: pineapple, pears, oranges… I felt like I was at the dinner scene with the Lost Boys in Hook.

It's a little different being up north. Ever since I hit Pennsylvania most locals I meet speak with accents. In my mind everybody sounds like they are from NY or NJ. The towns are beautiful and historic with old inns and houses and shops.

The Deer Head Inn across the street had a live

jazz jam session going on in the restaurant downstairs and me and four other thru hikers including Mr. Fabulous went to check it out. We all talked about different strategies for getting into New York City from the trail. You can take a train right into Grand Central Station on the Metro North line but it only runs on weekends, or you can hitch to another station where it runs all week. OR there are some bus options. I think I'll just figure it out when I get there. I might make it into NYC for the Fourth of July. Probably not heading out super early tomorrow because I still need to resupply. Goodbye PA! Hello NJ!

CHAPTER 4: NEW ENGLAND

Day 62

Location: Crater Lake

AT Mile: 1307.5

Miles Hiked Today: about 20

Was thinking of hiking farther today but came across an amazing lake about 7 pm and me and a few other thru hikers decided to go for a swim and stay the night. There are four of us here tonight.

Made it to New Jersey today! Crossed the border first thing this morning when I walked over the Delaware River Bridge. Extremely hot for hiking. Somewhere about 94 degrees. I've found the heat to be more mentally draining than any other factor thus far. I stopped at the first stream crossing I came to and washed my face and took my shoes off and soaked my feet for a few minutes. Thru hiker Cat Nap was there and we had lunch together.

Stopped by the Mohican Outdoor Center during the hottest part of the day to buy a soda. Saw a family who had been section hiking and who stayed with us at the church hostel. Moses, the father, thru hiked in 2002. His wife Peach and son Bear Bait are doing 1 month sections a year with him now until they section the whole trail. They were hiking with a weenie dog named Moxy. Bear Bait is only eleven years old and he's hiked just as much of the trail as I have. Impressive.

Beautiful sunset by the lake this evening that we watched over dinner. I made ramen noodles and threw in a packet of sliced pepperoni. We had an uninvited guest soon after that… A black bear that came up out of the woods and sniffed the air while watching us eat. He hung around for most of the evening, clearly not afraid of us. I had heard that the bears in New Jersey had become more of an issue recently and I guess the rumors are right. That's the ninth bear I've seen this trip but only the second that didn't run, not counting the mother with the cub up the tree since she had no choice. New Jersey has been hot and eventful so far…

Day 63

Location: High Point Shelter

AT Mile: 1332

Miles Hiked Today: 24.5

Stopped at Brink Road Shelter for lunch today. Where PA was just rocks, NJ gives you a little taste of everything. A few climbs, some more rocks and even some muddy stretches. Much more views compared to PA.

I could tell I was deep in Jersey territory today when I passed two older guys and they were telling me about the road crossing ahead. "When you cross that road you'll see a baah…"

I said, "I'll see a what?" He said "A baah, you know with drinks and food and stuff."

When I made it to the top of Sunrise Mountain I met a nice couple under the pavilion, Gary and Mary, who were up for a picnic and to see the view. They gave me two cold sodas and some snacks. We talked for a while before I headed out. Perfect trail magic timing for me because I had missed the previous water source and was incredibly thirsty. They really saved me.

There's a ridge runner camping beside our shelter tonight. He thru hiked last year and we talked about our trips. These guys work for the ATC and actually "patrol" the trail in certain areas. Hiking the AT is kind of their job. They love to stop and chat and they always have great info on the surrounding trail and upcoming towns.

Possible thunderstorms tonight, hope all that ends by morning hiking time.

Exposed boardwalk in New Jersey

Day: 64

Location: Vernon, NJ - Episcopal Church Hostel

AT Mile: 1350.9

Miles Hiked Today: 18.9

The heat is reaching unbearable levels. It's hard to believe it's 93 degrees and I'm all the way north in New York. I had planned to hike 5 miles farther today but when I heard about the hostel and showers and laundry and couches and sodas... I ended up hitching in and taking one of the longest and most enjoyable showers of the trip thus far.

I crossed a long boardwalk that stretched almost a mile through an exposed swamp. No tree cover, nothing but sun. A surprising amount of trail today traversed fields and farmland and even along some paved roads.

There's a thru hiker staying with us tonight who graduated from Chapel Hill last year. He went to North Stanly High School not far from where I grew up. His trail name is Bullet. We talked about the Triangle area of North Carolina and what a small world it is on the trail.

A lady from the church came by and brought Italian ice and put boxes of it in the freezer. We all got very excited. That's one thing the trail is about: learning to appreciate the small things. I guess it's debatable if Italian ice is a small thing on a day like today.

I want to be hiking before 6 am tomorrow. The early morning is the most desirable time to hike in this weather.

Day 65

Location: Buchanan Mountain, NY!

AT Mile: 1373.9

Miles Hiked Today: 23

Today was one of those days on trail that I know I will always remember. I left the hostel around 6:15 am and started trying to hitch back to the trail. Took longer than usual. I've noticed since I entered NJ that picking up hitchhikers doesn't seem to be as popular as down south.

I got a ride eventually and by 10 am I hit the NY border. It always feels good to hit another state. This will be my 9th state on trail.

Just passed the border I stopped to have a brunch on Prospect Rock, the highest point on the AT in NY. Lakes below me were shimmering like diamonds in the sun and a cool breeze blew steadily. It was then that I realized I could see the NYC skyline off to the east. What a surprising view to have during lunch alone on the Appalachian Trail.

NY didn't waste any time getting downright tough. The woods are a dense medley of intertwined rocks and roots and really difficult, short climbs. The trail twists and winds its way over exposed glacial rock, never giving you a view of what's just ahead of you. It almost feels claustrophobic because you know you're in the wilderness but everything is tangled so close around you. It was almost like the Smokies without all the moss. At one point I even climbed a wooden ladder that was placed next to a steep rock to get up it.

About five miles after the skyline view I crossed a road where an ice cream creamery was just around the corner. I sat there eating a cherry milkshake when Yoda, the thru hiker I hiked with in Virginia walks up. I hadn't seen this guy since the

Shenandoah! Almost 500 miles ago. I had communicated with him via Facebook so I knew he was close but I wasn't sure where. We had so much to catch up on. We talked about all the same places we had stayed and people we both knew and had met since we had last seen each other. We hiked on together and tented on top of Buchanan Mountain. We plan to hike together for the next few days until I get off on Thursday to go into the city. Was cooler today and such an eventful day on trail.

Day 66

Location: Tented at Graymore Spiritual Life Center

AT Mile: 1404.1

Miles hiked today: about 31

Big day today with Yoda. Night hiked the last mile with our headlamps on and it's 10:36 pm now so this will be short. It's way past hiker midnight. Hiking at night was a first for me. Didn't expect to see so many fireflies this far north but they sparkled in the fields and edges of the woods.

We couldn't find this religious center when we rolled in and spent about thirty minutes just walking around in the dark looking. Finally we stumbled upon it and there were so many people already asleep in the shelter that we decided to tent. Setting up the tent in the dark was difficult. The ground was full of rocks and my stakes didn't want to go in.

Hard day with steep climbs alongside Yoda. Reminds me of GA and NC in places. Crossed the Hudson river on a giant bridge. Saw more views of NYC, this time about 20 miles closer. We are only about 30 miles away. A cool thing about being this close to an enormous city is I get excellent phone service everywhere on trail.

The trail went through a small zoo near a road and we were looking forward to going through it but the zoo was closed. We had to settle for taking a bypass trail around it that was technically blue blazed. I probably only missed a few hundred yards of the white blazes but this is the first time I've had to use a blue blazed trail. It's still considered an alternative route for the AT though so I don't feel too bad. I also didn't walk any less by taking it and we weren't taking it with intentions of making a shortcut. It was just necessary.

Tomorrow will be my last full day on the trail until I go into NYC Thursday. Happy 4th of July!

Day 67

Location: Poughquag, NY

AT Mile: 1435.2

Miles Hiked Today: 31.1

Most painful day on trail to date. Woke up to rain coming down on my tent. When we headed out it stopped but the humidity made the air feel like misty soup. By 8 am our clothes were drenched in sweat to the last stitch.

I fell twice today. That's not normal for me. Once this morning on my side because the rocks were wet. Bent my trekking pole and my leg was bleeding. I was able to bend my pole back straight. The second time was this evening and I fell straight forward on more rocks. This one happened so fast I'm not sure how it even happened. Bruised my elbow pretty bad and it was swollen for the rest of the day.

This terrain isn't meant for doing 30 mile days but I wanted to give myself an easy 10 for tomorrow to get to the train station. A big problem with doing big miles through big climbs in hot weather is this: salt from sweat. It builds up on your body and begins to rub things raw. I had some of the most painful chafing I've had on trail by the end of today. When I finally got a shower later it burned to the point I couldn't even enjoy the shower. And I've enjoyed every shower thus far I've managed to get out here.

An awesome thing about the trail is you can go from having your worst experience to your best in the blink of an eye. As we were trying to hitch into town and it was getting dark fast, a couple in a truck picked us up. They ended up taking us out to dinner and treating us to burgers. THEN they told us we could stay at their house, get showers and do laundry. Unbelievable! As a kid that grew up in the heartland of NC and always heard the rumor that folks from up north were cold and harsh, I didn't expect the locals here to be this generous to hikers. I guess I'm learning that stereotypes aren't always true.

We're still sleeping on our inflatable pads in an empty bedroom but it sure beats the bugs and there's nothing like being clean.

Day 68

Location: New York City!

AT Mile: 1442.8

Miles Hiked Today: about 7.4

Yoda and I got back on the trail this morning knowing this could be the last time we see each other on our adventure. I was going into New York City until Sunday and he was hiking on. We made the Appalachian Train Station by 11 am. I was so glad to be done for the day and to have a few zeros ahead of me to take. The last few days have taken their physical toll.

Yoda and I said our goodbyes and I called a cab to take me to Pawling, NY where I bought a round trip ticket into Grand Central Station for about $24. I couldn't use the Appalachian Station on Metro North because it only runs on weekends. That's convenient for my return though because I'll be getting dropped off right where I left the trail.

The train ride took about two hours. The country gradually turned to concrete and looming apartment buildings as we neared the city. When I walked out of the train into Grand Central I experienced what I guess is called culture shock. Everything is so fast. So many people, many staring at my pack and hiking poles looking completely bewildered. I had to wait about 15 minutes until my friend from NYU, Caroline, met me and we took another train to her apartment in East Village, an area between uptown and the financial district where much of NYU is located. We haven't seen each other in years so it was fun to catch up on everything that has been going on in our lives since we last met. I showered and washed my clothes then we walked to a really popular burger shack (I later discovered this was Shake Shack, and at this point they were still only in New York) where I sunk my teeth into greasy cheeseburger deliciousness. Followed that with a frozen custard with roasted peaches.

We walked across town to a ferry that took us across the East River to Brooklyn where ET was being shown on an outdoor screen that overlooked the Manhattan skyline. We met one of her college friends, Megan, who watched the movie with us. You could even see the Statue of Liberty from the park. It was all very surreal to me after being on trail for so long.

I'm amazed at how easy it is to take the subway so quickly anywhere you please. We used it to get back to Manhattan from Brooklyn. This is my first experience with efficient public transportation.

Tomorrow we plan to visit Central Park and I'm going to check out a local REI for a few new gear items. Hiking is fun but being a tourist sure is fun too. This city is so alive like no place I've ever been before. Can't wait to experience more of it in the days to come.

Day: 69

Location: NYC

Miles Hiked Today: Zero!

My first zero day in over 600 miles. I plan to take one more tomorrow before heading back to the trail Sunday morning. Caroline has been so generous letting me stay in her apartment and showing me the city. She had to work until 1 pm today so I headed out on my own around 10 am to find the REI. It was about a 25 minute walk from her apartment. I ended up buying a new bandana there, new waterproof case for my phone and a lighter, and a more breathable pair of hiking boxer briefs. Caroline lives near Greenwich Village which was intriguing to walk through. The village used to have much of the culture of NYC, but I'm not sure how much is left. Still, many wealthy locals live here and tourists tend to stay farther uptown.

From REI I walked to Union Square. It was a hot day so I got an iced coffee at Starbucks and explored some of the nearby streets. Picked up a carton of strawberries from a Whole Foods market then sat under a tree in the square and ate the whole thing.

Caroline met me when she got off work and we took the subway to Central Park. I didn't expect the park to be so big. Everyone must say that. On the way back we stopped by a market and got supplies to make tacos. About five of her friends came over and we made dinner.

Having such a wonderful time in NYC that I don't really want to go back on the trail. Can't wait for another day tomorrow. The legs and feet are loving the time off from the trail.

Day: 70

Location: NYC

Zero Day

Taking my last zero in NYC today before I catch the train back to the trail tomorrow morning. Today was record breaking heat in the city. I headed out on my own this morning to check out St Marks Place and a nearby flea market. Also bought enough resupply for one day to get me to Kent, CT. I didn't want to purchase multiple days at city prices. Two things have saved me in the city: McDonalds and my iPhone. McDonalds because I can eat cheap and my phone because its Google maps feature is amazing for navigating on foot around this place.

Later Caroline showed me around NYU and we went down to Battery Park to eat lunch within view of the Statue of Liberty. We checked out the 9/11 memorial, or what we could see of it since it's still under construction. Unreal to be walking around ground zero and imagining what pedestrians standing exactly where I was standing on 9/11 were going through.

We decided that since it was so hot we would just catch a movie instead of going to Coney Island. Madagascar 3 was our choice, the penguins never disappoint. We took the subway back and I made sure all of my belongings were packed up for when I leave tomorrow. Her roommate is from Maine and she had just returned from home. She brought back seven lobsters! I had originally planned on getting lobster in Maine when I finished the trail but I guess I'll have to go ahead and have some early.

Tonight we plan on checking out Times Square and a nearby surf bar where Mr. Fabulous, the hiker I met in Delaware Water Gap, is having a hiker party that he invited a bunch of thru hikers to. One of Caroline's friends is also having a rooftop party at their apartment. Never expected to have such a glamorous night on my trip… Tomorrow it's back in the woods.

White blaze painted by the trail

Day 71

Location: Kent, CT

AT Mile: 1461.2

Miles Hiked Today: 18.4

    Crossed over into CT today and said goodbye to NY. Woke up in the city this morning and headed to Grand Central where my 9:48 train was waiting. Caroline came with me to say goodbye and just like that I was headed back to the wilderness. By about 11:30 am I arrived at the Appalachian Trail Railroad Station.

    Walking out of NYC and onto the trail was just as much, if not more, of a shock than walking into the city the first time. Three nights and two zeros had me adjusted back to urban life in society, where water pours from faucets, you can shower daily, a soft bed is waiting every night and you don't have to rely on granola bars for food. Suddenly I was surrounded by fields and trees and had no AC. It took a while for me to mentally and physically adjust. My body was telling me hiking was the last thing it wanted to do.

Today was a little cooler but the climbs still had me drenched in sweat. I didn't see a single other thru hiker all day. Saw quite a few weekenders and families. I talked to Yoda on the phone and he's about two days ahead of me. He should be farther but he caught a fever shortly after we split and has only been doing 15's.

I made Kent, CT around 7 pm. Resupplied here for the next few days from a gas station. If you've never walked into a gas station and bought enough food to last you for two or three days, you should try it. It isn't easy. What you really end up with is junk food. I had some dried pasta from before NYC still left though and bought a stick of salami from a deli yesterday, so I didn't need too much from the gas station.

This town comes off as upscale. Things are expensive. Yoda told me other towns in CT farther north are the same if not worse. It was too late to head back to the trail after running my errands but luckily Yoda told me the church here lets hikers tent out if they ask the pastor who lives next door. I rang his doorbell and he showed me where I could pitch.

Trying to get back on the trail early tomorrow. Hard to believe I was in NYC just this morning. Hope to see more thru hikers and possibly even my first south-bounder. Yoda has already met a few in front of me. Goodnight from Connecticut!

Day: 72

Location: campsite near Housatonic River

AT Mile: 1486.3

Miles Hiked Today: About 24

I have an interesting stove. It's made from a cat food can. Hikers call them fancy feast stoves. You punch a pattern of holes around the top with a hole punch (experimentation is needed to determine the proper amount of holes for optimum efficiency). I made three before I got one that worked really well. You pour denatured alcohol into the can, light it on fire, then place your cooking pot on top. I also use a wind screen not shown. Boils water in about six minutes.

Today I saw a couple other thru hikers and hiked with one by the name of Sparrow for about five miles. He thru hiked the PCT last year. He knew all about edible plants along the trail and was showing me what's good to eat. The other thru hiker I met was named Juggles. He knew and had met my friend Daffy from Raleigh that I passed back in Buena Vista, VA.

I'm now on my last section (3 of 3) in my guidebook. I had mom mail it to NYC. Even though I've done 2/3 of the trail I still have some of the hardest terrain ahead of me. Looking at the elevation profiles for NH and ME almost made me sick. The White Mountain National Forest, dubbed "The Whites" by thru hikers, are very serious hiking. The second highest peak on the whole trail is Mt. Washington located in the Whites. Alpine conditions are inevitable and weather can pose serious threats to hikers. I'm excited to make it that far but I'm also slightly nervous about navigating it.

Tomorrow I'm hoping to make Great Barrington, a large town about 30 miles from here. There's a hiker hostel that I might utilize but I may also just tent somewhere near on the trail. Hope I can get in there early enough to give me a few options.

Day: 73

Location: Great Barrington, MA

AT Mile: 1516

Miles Hiked Today: 29.7

Today I met Bearwalker and Buttons. They are trail angels and former thru hikers who live in Great Barrington, letting thru hikers stay at their house for free! Bearwalker thru hiked the AT southbound in 2008 and Buttons was a northbound thru hiker like me in 2010. Their house is decorated inside like a scrapbook, covered in AT related photographs, drawings and maps. They are such kind people.

I left Connecticut and entered Massachusetts today. I climbed more today than I have in a long time. Mt. Everette ascended 700 feet in just half a mile. I was at the highest elevation today that I've been at since Virginia. I met a couple on top of Mt. Everette from Cary, NC. The husband had just retired and they were on vacation.

I hiked with Sparrow again today. He's an ultralight backpacker like me. Unfortunately water was scarce for the last ten miles and we both went dry. All of the sources in my guidebook were just mud when I crossed them. To add to our discomfort the mosquitoes were viscous. Haven't seen them this bad yet. I probably had thirty land on me in the last five miles, even when I was moving. Big ones like I've never seen before. They even got me through my shirt. There was no stopping them.

When we got to the road crossing there was a cooler with trail magic in it. Cherry Pepsi! I haven't seen sodas in a cooler in a long time. For the most part now all the coolers we pass are empty. There's nothing like seeing a cooler for trail magic on a hot day and opening it to find only empty water bottles and empty cans.

On the cooler was Bearwalker's information and we called him right away. He came straight and picked us up. His hiker room is also his art studio and he has a desktop computer in it as well that he lets hikers use. I showered and walked down the block for pizza. Two other hikers are staying here as well, DW and Smiles. I actually gave Smiles his trail name about a week ago! He's section hiking NY to NH and I saw him before I went into NYC. Taking time off allowed him to catch back up. It's nice to see people I've met before, which wasn't happening when I was going fast.

Everyone decided to go watch the new Spiderman downtown so I tagged along. That's my third movie on trail… I might be going for some kind of record here. Hanging out with thru hikers is fun at this point. We've all come so far along the same trail that there's a lot to bond over. People we know, past terrain, upcoming trail rumors, which towns had the best ice cream (warning: talking about food potentially opens up a wormhole of endless conversation).

Tomorrow morning is laundry and resupplying before I get back on trail. On my 11th out of 14th state now. After Connecticut only Vermont, New Hampshire and Maine will remain.

Playing in rain shells to escape mosquitoes

Day 74

Location: Shaker Campsite

AT Mile: 1533.5

Miles Hiked Today: 17.5

Sparrow, Wall-E, DW and I played a few card games before dark on a wooden tent pad at Shaker campsite.

Today got off to a late start. Bearwalker dropped me off at the laundromat and by the time I did laundry and resupplied it was almost 10 am. Sparrow had cooked a big breakfast of eggs and potatoes when I returned to gather my gear so I ended up staying even longer to eat. I didn't hit the trail until about 11 am.

Wall-E is from CT and his mother drove up to do trail magic at a nearby road crossing with him today. We crossed their magic about six miles in. Pancakes, eggs, sausage, sodas, watermelon, bagels, muffins… A magical trail feast. I immediately regretted eating so much when I started the next climb. All my body wanted to do was go back to sleep, not hike.

All of us decided to do a short day and camp at the Shaker campsite listed in our guidebook. It's not a shelter but it has a bear box for storing food and a privy. I'm tented out along with the other thru hikers. I bet I've stayed in my tent more times in the last two weeks than I did in the first two months. I used to love shelters before it got hot. Now the mosquitoes have driven us all to seek refuge behind the safety of our no-see-um mesh. We all fought them off today while playing cards. We were all wearing our long-sleeved rain gear. It wasn't raining, but just provided another layer against the swarm. At one point I even had DW's pack cover wrapped around my legs. They still managed to find ways in.

The trail has been rugged but the largest climbs we keep hearing about ahead of us haven't started yet. Highs have been in the mid to lower 80's and although it's warm it is nothing like the heat I had to deal with in PA and NJ. Hoping those 90+ degree days stay away for a while.

Day: 75

Location: Dalton, MA - The famous trail angel Thomas Levardi's house

AT Mile: 1564.1 (or 620.1 from Katahdin)

Miles Hiked Today: about 31

Super enjoyable day today on trail. The terrain was mild with the exception of two 1,000 ft climbs early on that I knocked out while it was still cool. Today was the last of the "easy days" though. Tomorrow I'll face Mt. Greylock, the largest climb I've seen in about 700 miles. Elevation profiles from here onward are a new animal, the New England that I've only read about.

The other hikers I stayed with last night decided to stop at Goose Pond cabin this morning and take out the complimentary canoe. I kept going hoping to make it a big day. I'm glad I did because I got to meet two very generous trail angels. First, The Cookie Lady, a woman who lives just off the trail and has been making cookies for hikers for over 30 years! It was like something out of an enchanted Disney film to step off the AT to her cottage in the woods with free homemade cookies. I talked to her and her husband, a sweet couple. I also scored a coke and a Klondike bar.

Five miles later I crossed a road with a cooler sitting beside the trail. Ice cold Gatorades. I don't know who flipped the trail magic switch in Massachusetts but I'm liking it! I got practically nothing in

PA through NJ.

To top it off, I was overwhelmed with the hospitality of Mr. Levardi, a man that allows thru hikers to tent in his yard in Dalton. He's been doing this since 1975. When I arrived he came out to greet me and gave me a giant bowl of mint chocolate chip ice cream with whipped topping. It looked like one of those $15 desserts from a gourmet restaurant. There are thirteen thru hikers here tonight including myself and he's letting ALL of us sleep inside. Every room in his house has small mattresses or sleeping pads spread out across the floor.

I decided to get a cheese steak for dinner and Mr. Levardi let me borrow his bike. When I returned I stayed up past hiker midnight with a few other hikers and Mr. Levardi, looking at all of his photos from previous year's thru hikers. It's amazing to see hikers from the 80's, what they wore and what gear they had. I liked looking at the Katahdin summit photos from recent completions as well.

Some days really make you fall in love with the trail and the community that surrounds it. Today was one of those days tenfold.

Day: 76

Location: Sherman Brook Campsite

AT Mile: 1589.2

Miles Hiked Today: 25.1

Got up this morning and had coffee with Mr. Levardi while most of the other hikers were still sleeping. Thanked him, signed his register, then headed out the door around 7:30 am. I was anxious and excited about having a new, famous mountain to climb.

Nine miles into the day I crossed a road where I could see a Shell station just around the bend. I walked there and had one of my favorite convenience store combinations: a root beer, a pint of strawberry ice cream and a banana.

The climb up Greylock was big but gradual. I ascended for almost three hours. The summit was rewarding even though there were clouds out. On a clear day I was told you can see five states from the summit. There were quite a few tourists around and an expensive restaurant where I watched people pay $10 for a cheeseburger. I chose to sit out front eating goldfish crackers.

On the way down the north side of Greylock I met my first southbound thru hiker. We stopped and talked for a few minutes. He started May 30th. I don't plan on it taking me as long to do what he's covered since then though. For one I have my trail legs, stamina and body now after 1500 miles. Likewise I imagine he will do GA, NC and TN considerably faster than I did.

I made it to this marked campsite around 7:30 pm. It was empty and I prepared to spend the night alone in my tent. Just before dark a couple hiked in and they're spending their first night on the trail. It reminded me of my first night on the AT back a few years ago in NC when I was so excited to be on the trail with dad. It was back then that I had decided to eventually attempt a thru hike.

Tomorrow I'll get my breakfast in Massachusetts and my lunch in Vermont.

Day 77

Location: Goddard Shelter

AT Mile: 1616.1

Miles Hiked Today: 26.9

Long hot day but I hit the Vermont border early around 8 am. The border also marks the start of the Vermont Long Trail, a trail that starts here and continues on up to Canada. For the next 100 miles or so the AT and the Long Trail coincide.

Passed some impressive beaver ponds this morning. I've seen much more of their activity since passing NY. It's astonishing the scales they are capable of building to.

At one point today I was walking just a foot or so from a large pond where the whole bank next to me had been built up with wood and sticks. The water level of the pond was above grade near my knees but I was walking on dry planks placed by trail volunteers.

Met another south-bounder today in a shelter where I stopped for lunch. It's interesting to think that collectively we have thru hiked the entire trail exactly as we stand. To the foot, nothing more nothing less. I shared with him my knowledge of southern towns and caretakers that were very helpful. He told me about his experiences in the White Mountains. Even though a Nobo at this point has hiked a lot more of the trail than a Sobo, there is still a mutual respect. Sobos have completed the most difficult portion of the trail which still lies ahead of me.

Have one big climb in front of me tomorrow: Stratton Mountain. I've heard its difficulty should not be understated.

Day 78

Location: Manchester Center, VT - Green Mountain Hostel

AT Mile: 1646.1

Miles Hiked Today: 30

Had an inspiring view while eating breakfast. There was a firetower on the summit just north of the shelter I stayed at last night. Thru hikers like to say that we eat in places with views where they would charge you $10 for a peanut butter and jelly sandwich. We get to eat breakfast, lunch and dinner in a different spot every day for months.

Did not feel like doing 30 miles today but I had

called a hostel in Manchester Center yesterday and reserved a bed so I locked myself in to making it. Flies were bad today. Horse flies that try to latch on and buzz around your head for miles, sometimes two or three at a time. At times it feels like the most annoying thing I've ever experienced. Then they bite if they land on your neck or arm.

Stratton mountain was a tough climb. It was on that summit that Benton MacKaye first conceived the idea for the AT. I blew right over it without stopping, determined to make town before rain hit. Dark clouds had been looming all morning.

A light rain started before I made the road. By the time I emerged from the woods it turned into a downpour. I stood on the shoulder of the road thumbing for a hitch, drenched. Nobody stopped and I couldn't blame them. Twenty minutes passed and a southbounder emerged from the opposite side. As soon as he joins me a car stops. His name was The Natural and he is section hiking Vermont.

We went to the outfitter then to McDonalds. I couldn't eat enough to satisfy me. I bought a frozen pizza and brought it back to the hostel to make later.

I have my own bed here. Met a handful of other hikers: The Rhymenocerous and Often Awesome. The Natural is from Maine and he maintains a section of trail there. We stayed up late while he told us juicy info about the trail ahead in Maine.

Service has been off and on lately so I have

had trouble posting my blog. When I can't post I always save it and post later when I can. Sometimes it may be the next day or even two days later.

Drying clothes in an AT shelter

Day: 79

Location: Big Branch Shelter

AT Mile: 1662.6

Miles Hiked Today: about 15

Tried to do an easy day out of town but ended up getting soaked in rain. The Rhymenocerous tried stopping to dry his clothes alongside mine in a shelter.

The woods today were mystical, like hiking through a constant grove of Christmas trees and they smelled so sweet. The terrain is much more mountainous and I can tell that I'm getting closer to the New Hampshire and Maine wilderness. It feels much more remote and actually resembles the pacific northwest. Encountering so many large ponds lately, larger than any ponds I've ever seen before. There's lots of mud too and the rain didn't help. I talked to one hiker who fell today and I slipped a few times on roots and rocks.

I ordered what should be my last pair of trail runners last night from the hostel's computer and had them shipped to the post office in Hanover, NH. That's only about 100 miles north of here so I hope they arrive this week. Those should get me to the end in Maine.

Day 80

Location: Governor Clement Shelter

AT Mile: 1685.3 (or 498.9 miles from Katahdin)

Miles Hiked Today: about 22

Third consecutive day of rain. Had the scariest moment yet this evening. More like scariest hour. The last three miles of trail for me today was supposed to be a road walk detour due to damage from hurricane Irene last year. I had talked to a few southbounders who said to ignore the detour and do the trail, that it was clear, just required a few stream fords and that it was actually really neat to see the damage. So I tried just that.

Started the last three miles around 7 pm, knowing I could do three miles an hour and be at the shelter by 8. It didn't take me long to realize that this pace wouldn't be possible. Debris filled the stream crossings and some parts of the trail were rerouted on small side trails that were hard to find. To make things worse a storm rolled in midway. The sky grew darker. Visibility continued to dwindle. By 8 pm it was too dark to hike without headlamp in the woods where thick pine trees blocked out the sky. Rain poured on me and lightning flashed as I searched in my pack for my headlamp. I continued on. Rain flew through my beam of light and into my eyes, bright, like driving in the snow at night with your headlights on. I slipped on wet roots and mud as I stumbled down the trail.

Sometimes shelters are marked on side trails and I thought it was possible that I had already passed the shelter. Was I actually walking farther away from safety? Surely I had gone three miles by now? All this was running through my mind as I continued to get soaked.

After what seemed like forever I came to a clearing that the last of the sky's light lit up and there it was. I have never been so glad to see a shelter this summer. Most of the other hikers were already in their bags for the night but they managed to make room for me.

I guess I learned a lesson today but I'm grateful things didn't turn out worse. Vermont hasn't been that much fun. Flies, rain and mud. Looking forward to NH.

Day: 81

Location: Stealth camped north of Stony Brook

AT Mile: 1708.9

Miles Hiked Today: 23.6

Woke up and put on sopping wet socks, shirt and shorts. Had a big climb from the start that put me near 4,000 ft. Everything was wet from the night's rain and mossy roots and rocks caused me trouble on the way down the north side. I slipped and fell yet again before making it down. Every time I slip or trip up I think that could have been it. I could have ended this whole trip right there just like that with an injury.

Met a young thru hiker today named Gorp. We hiked the second half of the day together. We had heard of an inn just off the trail with a good Irish pub and restaurant and decided to check it out. I got to the road first and was preparing to hitch when a big bus pulled up out of nowhere. The driver asked us if we wanted a ride into town free of charge. It happened so fast. A welcome break from all the hard hitches I've had to conjure lately.

We ate and got another ride back fairly easily. Decided to stealth camp together past the last shelter of the day and do another three or so miles. Stealth camping means tenting somewhere in the woods that isn't a campsite. It requires finding a flat enough area to pitch which can be tough in the mountains at times.

Over 1700 miles hiked now. By Friday I should be in NH, my 13th state. Starting to feel tired but not in the traditional way. More of a combination of all the things that are going on. Starting to wonder if the prolonged physical stress of having to get up and push my body the same way every day is adding up to something. I hope that New Hampshire's White Mountains can rejuvenate my spirits.

Day 82

Location: West Hartford, VT

AT Mile: 1732.2

Miles Hiked Today: 23.3

Hiked with Gorp all today. It made time go by much faster and the climbs hurt less. Our conversations about music and books kept our minds occupied. Very cool temps today. I actually started the day hiking in long sleeves. Last night I was wrapped up tight in my mummy bag with the hood cinched over my head. Hard to believe that just a few weeks ago I couldn't sleep because I was sweating in my bag.

We hit two general stores today that were both only 0.2 miles off the trail. One had amazing organic ice cream. We feasted on meatballs, sharp cheese, fruit and soda. Got some beautiful views of the countryside while hiking through hay fields on top of mountains.

We made West Hartford by 7 pm and had dinner at the general store. Usually days on the AT aren't filled with this much town food. It was nice though because I didn't need to carry much food in my pack at all today. The owner of the store told us about Steve and Cathy, a couple who let hikers tent behind their house. We showed up and they were very welcoming. We hung out on their porch talking about the hurricane damage they took on last year. They said they got about 20 inches of rainfall and severe flooding. I believe it because almost every AT footbridge over a stream in Vermont no longer exists. You can see where they used to be and now we end up having to climb down and back up the other side to get across.

Tomorrow I leave Vermont for good and enter New Hampshire, the second to last state. Hanover, a town in NH just 10 miles from here, has shoes waiting for me at the PO so I plan to make it an easy day. Loving this cool weather. In much better spirits today!

Day 83

Location: Tigger's Tree House, Hanover NH

AT Mile: 1742.1

Miles Hiked Today: Only about 10 (I call this a nearo!)

 Hiked into Hanover today with Gorp and reached the NH border just before town on a large bridge spanning the Connecticut River. A piano was there on the North side and we played around on it a bit and celebrated reaching New Hampshire. Coming into town I did part of the longest road walk on the AT: five miles.

 Dartmouth College greeted us as we entered town, a lovely campus. Felt strange to be back on college grounds. Hanover is very hiker friendly. Many stores give thru hikers free things. I got a free slice of pizza from a pizza shop and sat across the street drying my down sleeping bag on the sidewalk in the sun. Since I've started tenting more lately the condensation has really started to make my sleeping bag damp from brushing against the walls of my tarp. I don't want it wet for when I hit the whites because I will need all the warmth I can get.

 Gorp went to see the new Batman film and I walked around town and checked out the outfitter. Hung out in the library for a bit online. Called Tigger's Tree House and arranged for them to pick me up. They got me, took me to Wal Mart where I got a new camera card, then to the grocery store. We headed back to their house where they have two campers in the yard. I have my own to myself, electricity, AC (won't need it) a mattress, it's amazing. They let me shower inside their home and wash my clothes. I made a frozen lasagna dinner in their microwave that I had bought at Wal Mart.

Around 6 pm a female southbound hiker came in named Drifter. She started at Katahdin one month ago today. We talked about our favorite places on the trail, why we were hiking, special places North and South of us. We stayed up watching Juno on TV and I shared some of my strawberries with her that I bought earlier.

Another great day of adventure. It truly is starting to feel like an adventure at this point. Excited to be entering the Whites at last in a day or two. I've heard so much about them in my research. Can't wait to see them firsthand.

My shoes didn't arrive at the PO today but they are expected to be there tomorrow. Hope they are. If not I might have to bounce them forward to myself and pick up at another PO.

New shoes arrive for the last time

Day 84

Location: stealth camped

AT Mile: 1761.6

Miles Hiked Today: 19.5

    A wild start to the morning. My shoes hadn't come to the post office in Hanover but the tracking said they were in a town down the road. The post office told me they wouldn't be delivered until Monday. The caretakers from Tigger's Tree House offered to drive me to the other town to talk to the FedEx office, my package's carrier. When I got there they told me my shoes had just been delivered to the post office, so back we drove. Apparently the PO didn't know what was going on. Good news is I finally got my shoes. Bad news is I got a very late start. The caretakers took me out to breakfast at an all-you-can-eat buffet before I hiked on and even paid for my food. I couldn't thank them enough.

     I hiked out of town past the remaining areas of Dartmouth's campus. It's strange to see an AT blaze right next to an NCAA football stadium. The first 100 miles or so are maintained by the DOC: Dartmouth Outing Club.

     I hiked with my headphones in for the first part of the day, the first time in a while. I know I will leave the headphones in my pack to enjoy the White Mountains, so I figured I would enjoy it for now. The Beach Boys and Bob Dylan helped the climbs go by faster.

     At the top of Moose Mountain I ran back into Gorp. We hiked the rest of the day together. Saw more southbound hikers today than ever before. Most of them haven't seen a bear yet but have seen lots of moose in Maine. Likewise, us Nobos haven't seen any moose but more bears than you could shake a stick at. To us moose sound exciting. To Sobos, bears.

We are stealth camped just before Smarts Mountain with a southbounder named Shadow. Tomorrow we plan to get to the base of Mt. Moosilauke, the first of the White Mountains. We've heard names like Franconia Notch and Mt. Washington for a while now. They all seem mysterious and grueling. Hoping for good weather for my time through them. Looking to get a solid day of miles in tomorrow.

Day 85

Location: Jeffers Brook Shelter

AT Mile: 1786.4 (or 397.8 from Katahdin)

Miles Hiked Today: 24.8

Started hiking around 8 am and had two strenuous climbs immediately: Smarts Mountain and Cube Mountain. These were both two of the harder climbs I've had in many miles. I could definitely tell I am in NH and that I was getting closer to the White Mountains. In fact, most of the exposed rock that I hiked over today was very white.

Gorp and I said goodbye around lunch and I hiked on. He was stopping to cook food out of his mail drop from Hanover. Apparently he got lots of dinners in his mail drop so he is making them for lunch as well. He didn't plan on going as far as me so this might be the last time I ever see him.

Hit a road one mile south of this shelter and

tried to hitch into a town to pick up a few lunch / dinner items for tomorrow. Couldn't get a hitch after 30 minutes and it was starting to get dark. I didn't want to end up with another night-hiking adventure like I had back in Vermont so I decided to hike on. Luckily another hiker named Brock had too much food and gave me some snacks and pound cake to pack out so I should be fine until I can get into Lincoln, NH. I've been eating a lot of summer sausage lately but I've lost about 20 pounds on this trip so far.

I'm staying at the base of Mt. Moosilauke, the first White Mountain. Sleeping in the shelter tonight with three southbounders. One is from Winston Salem. It's interesting to listen to them converse among themselves. It reminds me of northbounders around NC/TN. All they want to do is compare gear and talk about who has the best. I don't remember the last time I heard a Nobo talk gear. We're sick of it by now. Who cares what the other person is carrying, both people are obviously doing something that works if they made it all the way to New Hampshire from Georgia.

Under 400 miles to go now. It's going to be one heck of a ride from here on out. Tomorrow I walk into the White Mountains.

Day 86

Location: Eliza Brook Shelter

AT Mile: 1802.3

Miles Hiked Today: 15.9

Woke to rain pattering softly on the shelter roof. Frustrated that it was going to rain my first day in the whites, I started up Mt. Moosilauke and the rain ceased but dark clouds still loomed. It felt like the longest climb of the entire trek to reach the summit. On top I sat alone, above tree line surrounded by rocks. Clouds obscured my view which was a shame because I had heard that Mt. Washington can be visible and even the Atlantic Ocean on a very clear day.

Climbing down was worse than climbing up. The trail followed a waterfall steeply for about a mile in which I descended 2,000 feet. I passed a sign which warned that this section of trail is extremely difficult and should not be done during wet or icy conditions. It was the steepest section of trail I've hiked yet. Rebar was built into the rocks in an attempt to provide footing. A big welcome to the whites.

When I hit the next road I decided to try my hand at getting into town to resupply. A group of people on a motorcycle trip came up and offered me a ride after talking to me about my hike, so I rode on the back of a Harley Davidson, no helmet, six miles into town with my pack on and poles collapsed. Can't imagine what I looked like. It was my first time on a motorcycle. At first I asked the burly bearded guy if I should hold on to the bike or hold on to him. He replied, "Don't hold on to me nowhere." And I followed suit.

The Price Chopper store had my favorite ice cream: Ben and Jerry's Willie Nelson's Peach Cobler. I also got lunch at a pancake house and called a shuttle to take me back to the trail after re-supplying.

The whites have proven to me this: I can't do the miles I averaged before through them. The difficulty of their terrain is not just all talk. The climbs are long, rocky and often exposed. Still haven't seen a moose :/

Day 87

Location: Liberty Spring Campsite

AT Mile: 1813.8

Miles Hiked Today: 11.5

Intense thunderstorms all night. The volume of the lightning strikes prevented me from sleeping well. Lots of rain fell overnight which swelled the brooks and streams I had to hike through today. One bridge was out so I was forced to ford and the water came up near my waist.

Today proved to me how dynamic the weather

is in the whites. 50 mph winds, rain and clouds slowed my pace. Dense fog for the first half of the day. Climbing South Kinsman mountain sent me through the most rugged terrain yet, clambering over car-sized pieces of granite to the summit. Visibility was extremely reduced and everything I touched was wet.

On the other side I took a break at Lonesome Lake Hut. This is the first hut I've ever been in. They have caretakers who make food for paying guests. There are many huts in the whites but they all are very expensive, $85 a night. Thru hikers sometimes can get work for stay. I hiked on.

Started climbing toward the Franconia Ridge, a famous, beautifully exposed and highly photographed two mile hike along one of the most famous stretches of the trail. Dark clouds were all around and I was concerned about having bad weather on the ridge so I stopped at this campsite a few miles before. Glad I did because I ended up cooking dinner under the vestibule of my tent while rain pounded my tarp. At 6 pm it was cold enough to see my breath. I was glad I wasn't on the ridge ahead. Supposed to be in the 30's here tonight. Hope better weather comes tomorrow for the exposed stretch.

Day 88

Location: Zealand Falls Hut

AT Mile: 1830.9

Miles Hiked Today: 17.1

Extreme alpine conditions over Franconia Ridge this morning. 50 mph winds. 70 mph were reported on Mt. Washington. Crossed the two mile exposed ridge with about 30 ft visibility. It has been the scariest thing I've encountered yet. My hands went numb from the cold. The clouds and wind were blowing so hard it was even difficult to breathe at times. Moreover, I missed out on seeing the view.

As the day went on temperatures rose and clouds faded. Made it to this hut and they are allowing me to work for stay along with three other thru hikers: Possum and Often Awesome (known as The Ape Team) and a thru hiker named Baked Beans.

I washed dishes while Possum cleaned the ice out of the freezer. The ice was stuck all in his beard when he finished. The crew here was playing Johnny Cash songs while we worked. We received leftovers; all the pork tenderloin we could eat, salad, peas and bread. Sleeping on the floor tonight in the kitchen. Tomorrow they are calling for rain.

Summit of Mt. Washington

Day 89

Location: Lakes of the Clouds Hut

AT Mile: 1850

Miles Hiked Today: 19.1

    Did my biggest day yet in the whites. Again poor weather conditions and low visibility obscured all views. Hiked down to route 302 and hitched to a general store to resupply with Possum and Often Awesome. Ace, the guy who picked us up, works at

Lakes of the Clouds hut. I would run into him later on that night in the hut.

The Noodleheads were at the general store when we arrived. I've been seeing them on and off for the past few days as well.

Started climbing up towards the Presidential Range, a group of high, exposed summits named after US presidents. Eisenhower, Jackson, Franklin, all very rocky and most in alpine conditions. Stopped at Mizpah hut then Baked Beans came along. We decided to hike the remaining five miles to Lakes of the Clouds, a hut only 1 mile from Mt. Washington. We went through the thickest clouds yet to reach it. Condensation formed quickly on my beard and clothes. Absolutely no visibility.

At the hut we were offered work for stay again. This time I had to clean out a giant grease pan. A little tougher than my last gig. Tomorrow we shoot to get over Mt. Washington. Calling for bad weather again. I've just started to accept it. At this point all I care about is good weather on Katahdin. I'll wait a week to get it before summiting if I have to.

Day 90

Location: Pinkham Notch, Gorham NH, Hiker Paradise Hostel

AT Mile: 1864.8

Miles Hiked Today: 14.8

The three month mark. It feels like just yesterday I was driving with Dad down to Georgia to start. Summited Mt. Washington in thick clouds this morning first thing. I wandered off the trail twice on the way up. At that elevation there are no trees and the maintenance club in charge of the trail doesn't blaze the rocks very often. Instead hikers follow cairns, or large stacks of rocks, some over six feet tall. We didn't see the visitor's center at the summit until we were about 15 ft away because of the cloud cover. Soon after we arrived lots of tourists started to pour in off the Cog Railway, a train that carries passengers to the summit. It has been a thru hiker tradition for many years to "moon" the railway but I restrained myself. In 2008 ten thru hikers were arrested for doing it.

As I was preparing to leave Washington the clouds started to disperse and i got somewhat of a view. I hiked the remaining miles of the Presidential Range alone. Clouds would thicken then blow away then thicken again.

Descending down to Pinkham Notch I dropped in elevation so much for so long that my hands and wrists were starting to hurt from my pole use. That is stress that would otherwise be transferred to my knees. My knees have felt swollen and sore since I entered the whites, an area of my body that I never really had problems with before.

Hitched into town, had homemade lasagna at a family restaurant called Mr. Pizza, had my trekking pole tips replaced at an outfitter / hardware store then walked a mile across town to this hostel. It's above the office of a motel. I was glad to see actual mattresses on the bunks as opposed to wooden planks. Might actually sleep in tomorrow and not push out early.

Only about 20 more miles of White Mountains to go! I should be in Maine in just a few days time.

Day 91

Location: Imp Shelter, the last structure in the Whites.

AT Mile: 1877.9

Miles Hiked Today: 13.1

The 7th straight day of bad weather. Poured rain for the last half of the day while I was doing a steep, two mile rocky descent down to this shelter. I was concerned about injuring myself and I passed a section hiker who was concerned as well. He has done over forty 4,000 footers in NH and he said that descent was one of the worst. It sure felt like a long two miles.

I'm almost done with the whites. I must say I won't miss them. By noon tomorrow I should be out of them completely. My 13 mile day today felt like a 25. My knees and feet are sore from hiking predominantly on exposed rock. I hear southern Maine is extremely difficult as well but I shouldn't have a climb as difficult as today until I summit Katahdin at the northern terminus of the trail.

Ran into Possum and Often Awesome at the last hut. I stopped for lunch. They were jealous of my sausage and egg McMuffin that I packed out of Gorham. If I had known all that rain was coming I would have probably tried to work for stay there but instead I rolled the dice and lost.

Staying at a pay shelter full of section and thru hikers. About 12 in total and the shelter is only supposed to hold ten. Reminds me of being packed like sardines in the Smokies back in NC. One of the section hikers shared a small bottle of wine he packed up with me and we sat under the awning of the shelter and watched the rain drops fall through the trees. He said he gets taunted about his large pack but other hikers are jealous of his wine glass that he never leaves at home.

Maine should be here before I know it. Hope it brings good weather with it. Vermont and New Hampshire both produced more rainy days than dry.

Day 92

Location: Gorham, NH

Second time at the hostel here

AT Mile: 1885.9

Miles Hiked Today: 8

Did a Nero today and I'm staying at the same hostel in Gorham as before, I just entered from a different road crossing. Feels strange to be back in the same town, almost as if I haven't gone anywhere although trail wise I have. Finished up the whites this morning in the rain. This was my 8th consecutive day of rain. The next shelter was another 17 miles and I knew regardless if I hiked on or not I will still reach Maine tomorrow so I decided to come into town and relax and dry out.

Saw a batting cage next to a putt-putt course and got a few tokens to take a few swings. It felt good to do something recreationally other than hike. Went to an all-you-can-eat Chinese buffet for lunch. It stayed cloudy and drizzling all day. The forecast tomorrow doesn't look much better but I plan to get out early, around 6:45 am.

Talked to a few college friends on the phone during my spare time today and we made plans for when I return. I even started working on my final blog post for this blog, the one that will accompany my summit picture (assuming I don't injure myself between now and then and don't finish).

Yoda is already halfway through Maine. I wish we could summit together. That's OK because I'm sure I will see him at Trail Days next year and also when he goes down south from PA to hike the Smokies again. Dad and I are also making plans for him to come up and summit with me. I still have a few weeks left but hitting Maine tomorrow sure will make everything feel like it's finally coming to an end. Tomorrow I enter my 14th and final state.

Day 93

Location: Full Goose Shelter

AT Mile: 1907.3

Miles Hiked Today: 21.4

    Had such an epic day today and ended my bad weather streak. This afternoon was gorgeous. Felt so great to look up and see that clear blue sky and feel the warmth of the summer sun again.

    The owner of the hostel, Bruno, drove me back to the trail this morning a 6:45 am sharp. Hiked for five hours without seeing anybody. Being out of the whites now there are no tourists and very few vacation hikers or day hikers. The trail was much less worn. That's the way I like it, authentic. I feel that's how the trail really wants to be.

    The problem was that since I was the first hiker out and didn't see anybody hiking south, I got every spider web from the night before. They seemed worse than usual. Every now and then I would spot them first but usually they just hit me right in the face.

Made the Maine border, my 14th and final state, around 3 pm. I've been telling people for so long that i'm hiking to Maine when they ask me and now I've actually done it. GA to ME is actually a reality now, not just a dream. Still, oddly, if I had to quit now I would feel just as unsuccessful as if I had quit in NY, or even an earlier state. There's still 270 miles of the AT left to hike, a very significant amount. Maine is the second longest state on the trail next to Virginia. Southern Maine is also one of the most difficult if not the most difficult sections of the trail.

I'm amazed at how difficult the terrain is. It now takes me twice as long to go as far as I could before NH. The downhills are littered with giant slabs of granite that are wet and slick from mountain springs. Today I had to climb multiple wooden ladders and rebar built into the rock to reach ledges where the trail continued on. With every step I know that one wrong move could end my hike immediately.

Tomorrow I will do what has been called the most difficult mile of the AT: the Mahoosuc Notch. It's a jumbled boulder pit one mile long that requires hikers to maneuver in odd ways. For most hikers it takes over an hour to complete. Just before the shelter I came across quite a few rocky balds that were stunning. I ran into Talks a Lot, a section hiker I stayed in a shelter with back in PA. She jumped up to do some of Maine. It's always interesting to see those I haven't seen in months.

Super excited to be in my final state. It's bittersweet to see the journey start coming to an end. I'm going to try and enjoy Maine as much as possible. Who knows if I'll ever get the chance to hike this area ever again.

Following Buzz and Gretel in Maine

Day 94

Location: Frye Notch Lean-to

AT Mile: 1922.8

Mikes Hiked Today: 15.5

    Beautiful weather but a demanding day on trail. The Mahoosuc Notch took me an hour and a half to complete. I fell very hard, my hardest fall yet, when I was only a few minutes in. My foot slipped on a small ledge and I landed directly on my back. Luckily my pack took most of the fall. I laid there a few seconds staring up in pain thinking for sure some part of me must really be damaged but i walked away with only a bruise and a few scratches. From then on I went through the notch very cautiously.

Some parts of the Notch required me to go under giant boulders and at times I had to take my pack off and push it through a narrow rock tunnel then crawl through after it. As soon as I finished the climb I faced the Mahoosuc Arm, one of the hardest climbs in Maine. It was much like what I faced in NH. I had to grab roots and trees, anything I could really, to pull myself up the climb.

I was given food four times today, a new record! First this morning when I made a true hiker swap with Talks-a-Lot. She needed ibuprofen and I was low on food so I gave her seven tablets in exchange for a granola bar, a small bag of trail mix and then she made me a peanut butter and jelly sandwich for breakfast. I also got a Capri Sun and a banana from a group I met in the Notch. When they found out I was thru hiking they started offering me things. The third time was coming down to Grafton Notch, a day hiker told me there were sodas and another banana in a cooler in the back of his jeep. While I was eating this, ANOTHER day hiker offered me brownies. It was one heck of a trail magic day and at the perfect timing too because I was really running out of food. I had been contemplating hitching in to a campground to try to resupply. Instead I was able to hike on.

Hiked the last part of the day with Buzz and his dog Gretel. I'm tented at the shelter with many other thru hikers. There was one spot left in the shelter but I decided to tent instead in hopes of a better night's sleep.

Word on the trail is there's a sort of cruise sickness going around amongst hikers in Andover. That's the town i plan to resupply in tomorrow. Everybody seems to know somebody who has gotten it. Yoda text me to warn me of Sobo's who could potentially have it. I hope to just hop in, resupply and hop out so hopefully I won't risk anything. Definitely not taking a night there to risk it.

Day 95

Location: Hall Mountain Lean-To

AT Mile: 1933.3

Miles Hiked Today: 10.5

More rain today that slowed me down and I ended up taking refuge in this shelter. The next shelter was quite a ways so I decided to end the day here with three other thru hikers: Stray Dog, Buzz, Nutterbutter and Chipmunk.

Went in Andover today and had a huge breakfast this morning. Bought a 12 pack of Dr. Pepper and brought it back to the trail crossing to put in the stream. Left a note that said "Love, Quicksilver". Later, while we were all in the shelter escaping the rain, thru hiker The Dude came up and said "Who is Quicksilver??" and gave me a big bear hug. He was super excited to have gotten a soda. I was glad I actually got to see someone who got some.

Wanted to get more miles under my belt today but didn't want to tent in the rain. I had a great time hanging out with this crew of thru hikers in the shelter though. We talked about our favorite hostels and states and places along the trail. Hoping to make tomorrow a bigger day.

Day: 96

Location: Sabbath Day Pond Lean-To

AT Mile: 1954.4

Miles Hiked Today: 21.1

Did my first 20 mile day today in Maine. It was the hardest 20 I've pulled all summer. My knees are the most tender area on my body now. Ever since NH they have been acting up. Hiked with Honey Badger, 23 year-old ex marine from Maryland. We're staying in the same shelter tonight with El Dog, a somewhat famous Whiteblaze.net poster who is now attempting a Sobo hike.

We sat in the shelter talking about Katahdin, the few towns between there and here, places we heard that were good to eat or stay. At this point I can pretty much plan out the rest of my hike. Tomorrow we will dip into Rangeley to eat and resupply. I laid in my bag and looked at the town map in my guidebook planning everything I wanted to do.

I would estimate that over half of the thru hikers in this area are getting a bad 24 hour stomach sickness. I've been trying to avoid contact by not touching trail logs and washing my hands with my liquid soap I keep in my pack.

Maine is HARD. Beautiful, the woods are so dark. The spruce trees are very black and even during the day if you look into the woods everything fades to black. Passed some very large lakes today that we're tempting. Ready for tomorrow and town food.

Day 97

Location: Piazza Rock Lean-To

AT Mile: 1965.6

Miles Hiked Today: 11.2

Did ten miles into Rangeley, ME. Resupplied and hopped back out to the next shelter north which wasn't far. In town Honey Badger and I went to Sarge's Pub and had lunch while watching the Olympic trials, then headed across the street to an ice cream stand where I found another favorite flavor: cotton candy. Did laundry at the laundromat and hung out in the library for a while. I was in no rush to get out of town because Saddleback Mountain is just up the trail and the next shelter is a ways over the summit. My plan is to go over tomorrow morning.

I was doing the math in the library to see when I should finish. I wanted to give dad an estimate to let him know when to come up. I think I should be in the last trail town before Katahdin on or near August 14th. That means I should summit by the 16th. Of course, I can't tell the future and anything can happen. Terrain and weather conditions will probably play the biggest part.

I think Mercury, the very fast ultralight hiker I hiked through TN to Damascus with, summited Katahdin today. Hoping to meet up with him sometime after our hikes to talk about our different experiences.

Excited about Saddleback Mountain tomorrow! Heard it's exposed and really enjoyable.

Day 98

Location: Crocker Corque Campsite

AT Mile: 1988.7 (195.5 from Katahdin)

Miles Hiked Today: 23.1

Another big day in Maine but had wonderful weather that allowed me to hike late into the afternoon. It's very common to get afternoon thunderstorms around 6 pm but none today. Summited Saddleback Mountain this morning and had gorgeous views of many Maine lakes all around. Still I haven't seen a moose. I really hope to spot one before I finish. Yesterday there was one mounted in the grocery store that was almost 900 lbs.

Felt more energized today because I carried more food than usual out of town yesterday. I've been taking breaks more often and consuming more calories. Still it's near impossible to take in more than I'm burning off.

Less than 200 miles to go now and only about 30 more miles of very difficult terrain before I hit the final stretch which has much less elevation change. The trade off for less elevation: mud. Also, bugs. There's a magical point on a big mountain that is below tree line but above the bug line. That's usually the nicest place to camp.

Passed a bronze plaque today that marked the spot where the last section of the GA-ME Appalachian Trail was completed in 1937. Tomorrow I should hopefully hit another important landmark: the 2,000 mile mark.

Felt pretty warm today. The sweat was pouring on the ascents. Tomorrow I will go into Stratton for part of the day to charge my electronic devices, eat and possibly resupply a few items although my food bag still feels pretty heavy.

Day 99

Location: Horns Pond Lean-To

AT Mile: 2,001.1 (that's 2,000 miles hiked!!!)

Miles Hiked Today: 12.4

2,000 mile mark was passed today. There was no sign, no physical indication or marker on the trail. I knew when I reached a viewpoint which was marked in my guidebook at 2000.3 that I had passed it 0.3 of a mile back. I had planned on celebrating at this view by taking a break and enjoying the lookout and peaceful surroundings but instead I found that a giant group of 15 year-old hikers were already enjoying the view. I hiked on.

Earlier today I hitched into Stratton, a tiny town, with Aspen, a thru hiker I met back in PA when I was doing a short side trail off the AT to reach a water source. I hadn't seen him since. We got dinner at the Stratton Diner and talked about running. He's a marathon runner and I've wanted to get involved in long distance running so I questioned him about his training techniques, schedule and diet. All while devouring homemade banana pancakes and a full course breakfast. We followed that up with ice cream from the general store where we both resupplied.

The southbounders I meet now are very different from those I first saw in Vermont. These look too fresh, unseasoned with no beard growth and a little extra weight to lose. They've only been on the trail for about two weeks. They tell us congratulations and we tell them good luck. Historically even less southbounders finish than northbounders. Usually only about one out of ten.

I stopped early at this shelter because clouds were starting to roll in. There was a great view of the next summit from this shelter but now it's completely covered in white, nothing left to see, as if the mountain uprooted itself and walked away. Winds are strong and even starting to blow white clouds into the shelter. Still, I'm glad I'm not in my tent.

This last tall range of mountains I started today and will finish tomorrow is called the Bigelows. They are steep, alpine and surrounded by lakes and large ponds. Hopefully clouds will clear tomorrow so I can enjoy them.

Sunny break by a deep blue Maine pond

Day 100

Location: Pierce Pond Lean-To

AT Mile: 2,029

Miles Hiked Today: 28.8

    Longest day I've done in weeks. After the first half of the day the elevation change mellowed out and I was able to increase my pace. Cloudy and cool all day but no rain. Summited Avery Peak and a few other exposed Bigelows early on and was rewarded with views into the valleys below.

    The shelter I'm beside tonight is right next to a very large pond. It was full when I arrived so I set my tent up right behind it while the sunset was blazing. Loons were bellowing and at first I mistook the sound for coyotes. Buzz and Gretel are both here and Buzz calls the Loons "coyotes of the water."

I am only three miles south of the Kennebec River crossing. It is too dangerous to ford so hikers are required to take a boat across operated by a caretaker who has a certain schedule of operation. He starts at 9 am so I will get to cross the river and go into Caratunk in the morning.

This pond is where the northbound thru hiker drowned earlier this year. There was a small memorial for him made out of a rock cairn and with a carved piece of wood that read his trail name. It's extremely sad what took place here and it puts a somber damper on an otherwise peaceful and stunning campsite. He was swimming from the same rock that I snapped a photo of the sunset from before bed.

It is a new era in my thru hike. The hardest terrain is behind me now. It's simply a matter of time and putting in the work needed to complete what's left of the trail.

Day 101

Location: Pleasant Pond Lean-To

AT Mile: 2038.7

Miles Hiked Today: a measly 9.7

The loons kept me up all night last night. I was cold in my sleeping bag and by morning I had both base layers on, my wool cap and the hood of my sleeping bag tightly cinched around my head. I was excited about getting to take the canoe ferry across the Kennebec River so I hopped up, ate what was left of my summer sausage for breakfast, packed up and hiked out.

Three miles later I reach the river. Another thru hiker named Two Cents was there waiting on the ferry. When it came we were required to put on life jackets. One of us had to help paddle and I volunteered. I felt that since I was in essence "aqua blazing" and not hiking this 70 yards of the trail the least I could do to help my guilty conscience was to donate manpower to get us across. Even so, the ferry service is the official way for thru hikers to cross the river. Hikers have drowned in the past trying to ford so it's strongly advised to use the service.

Once in town Two Cents and I walked to the Sterling Inn, 1 mile east. There I resupplied from their stock of trail food to get me to Monson. Also paid $7.50 to wash my clothes and shower without stay. This was my first shower in Maine. I went 140 miles (over a week) without showering. Needless to say I needed one.

While my clothes dried I sat upstairs watching TV and lounged on a leather couch. Flipping through channels I saw Keeping Up With The Kardashians was on. It reminded me of why I wanted to hike the trail in the first place. Such an incredibly different lifestyle and set of priorities and needs than those I currently live with on the AT.

Went to the Kennebec Pub and Brewery for lunch and had a BBQ burger with fries and a huge chocolate chip ice cream sandwich for desert. Had to walk most of the way back to the trail until an elderly couple picked me up and gave me tangerines to carry out with me.

The last five miles up to the shelter were miserable. I was so full from all the food I felt sick. I should have known better. I was thirsty but couldn't drink my water because I was so full. Multiple times I had to take breaks on rocks and fallen trees because I felt queasy. Was very glad to finally see the shelter.

Huge pond here as well and we sat out on the dock while the sun set with our feet in the water. Have the shelter to myself tonight because the other hikers are tenting. Can't believe I will finish the trail in only a week. I can't imagine a life outside of the trail right now.

Day 103

Location: Chairback Gap Lean-To

AT Mile: 2,095.7

Miles Hiked Today: 26

I've finished 26% of the 100 mile wilderness

with this 26 mile day. Had an all-you-can-eat breakfast this morning at Shaw's Hostel then was shuttled back to the trail by 8 am. Three miles into the wilderness it starts to rain. Came to a stream ford where I changed into my flip flops to cross. The hiker on the other side turned out to be "The Machine". I had heard about him recently and he had been hearing about me for months. He started May 7th. That's after me and Mercury, who has already summited. He's on pace to finish the trail the same day as me, his goal of 100 days even. We talked and found out we were shooting for the same shelter so we decided to hike together. I let him lead and found it difficult to keep up on the ascents but I managed.

Big thunderstorm rolled in while we were climbing Barren Mountain. We were both drenched. We hiked on in sopping wet clothes and shoes and socks, talking about mutual friends we had made and met at different times along the trail and whether they were still on the trail or quit.

We came to a ledge just before sunset and stopped to snack. Just then the clouds parted, lakes appeared below us out of nowhere and the sun inched out from behind the clouds and spilled its warm light on us. A moment that a picture just can't justify but will live on in my mind as a vivid memory of Maine. We sat there in our damp clothes soaking up the glow.

On the way down to the shelter it started to get dark. Hiked the last five minutes by headlamp. The shelter turned out to be full so I was forced to pitch. Just then, more rain. I feel as if I've gotten the worst weather at the most difficult parts of the trail. Hopefully my tent keeps me dry tonight.

Day 104

Location: East Branch Lean-To

AT Mile: 2116.4

Miles Hiked Today: 20.7

Woke up with puddles of rain water in my tent and my sleeping bag slightly wet. Rain all day. Hardest rain since the Shenandoah. Didn't get a photo because my phone was in my pack all day, safe in a zip-loc bag. Hiked with The Machine all day today. We passed The Bee Man hiking south. I met him at Standing Indian Shelter back in NC! He was doing a flip flop. The Machine had met him too back in the south. We stood there on the trail talking for about 15 minutes.

If you think hikers smell bad you should smell them when their socks and clothes have been soaked for days. Kind of reminds me of a high school locker room. We summited White Cap, the last big mountain before Katahdin. The guidebook boasts that a great view of Katahdin, the first real view of the mountain that a northbounder gets, is at the summit. We saw nothing but white clouds and rain. That's OK. I'll get to see it up close and personal when I'm climbing it.

From word of mouth it's supposed to be rainy and wet for the next two days, just as I should be finishing up the wilderness. Good news is it's supposed to be nice Monday and Tuesday. That's what matters to me now. Shelter is packed with eight of us in a six person lean-to. Just glad to be dry.

Day 105

Location: Wadleigh Stream Lean-To

AT Mile: 2146 (38.2 from Katahdin!)

Miles Hiked Today: 30

Third day of rain in the 100 mile wilderness. Still managed to push a 30 with The Machine despite chafing, mud and an army of mosquitoes. Trail was gradual today and we only had one real climb. Made good time to this lean-to by 5:30 pm.

Passed yet another flip flopper, Unicoi Zoom, that I had met down in Virginia at The Place hostel. It's so amazing to meet somebody again on the same trail as before but over 1,000 miles away. Feet took a beating today being soaked for so long. I changed into dry socks at night but after being in wet shoes for 12 hours they aren't a pretty sight.

I was joking earlier today about how awesome it would be to have a shelter to ourselves, having room to sprawl out and not worry about our gear being in somebody else's way. Somehow, when we arrived, we DID have the shelter to ourselves. Others here are tenting. One of the section hikers gave me a pack of decaf coffee that I made after dinner and The Machine found a candle. It almost feels like being in a living room. The shelters really do feel like home to me. I've met lots of hikers that don't like them but I love them. I've even come to terms with the mice… as long as they don't crawl across me in the middle of the night. tonight could be my last night in a shelter. A sad thought for me.

Tomorrow I hike 22.8 miles out of the wilderness and meet dad in Milinocket. The next day I have eight miles to do to the base of Katahdin. The next day, Tuesday, we summit with a five mile climb. That will be the end.

Day 106

Location: Millinocket, Maine: The Appalachian Trail Lodge

AT Mile: 2168.8

Miles Hiked Today: About 22

The Machine and I reached a summit this morning that was supposed to have a 16 mile line-of-sight-view of Katahdin. Instead we got fog. Still, not being able to see the end of the trail just makes the anticipation that much stronger.

Everything was damp today but we didn't get

rained on. I hiked on ahead of Machine to Abol Bridge, the end of the 100 mile wilderness. I ate my last pop tart nine miles before the road. If I had carried any less food I would have really been struggling.

As soon as I had service I called dad and was surprised to find he was already in Millinocket. He came to pick me up and gave me a big hug. It was strange to see and ride in my old car again. We drove to the lodge where I had made reservations and checked in, then went to a pizza house for dinner. I resupplied for the last time in the local IGA.

It feels like all play and no work now that I'm with dad. We're hiking about 10 miles tomorrow and summiting Tuesday. All my stuff is wet so I have it laid out on the porch drying. It's hard for ultralight hikers to stay light when tarps, socks and packs in general are soaked. I've been carrying a lot of water weight the last few days.

I was so ready to be out of the wilderness but I can't wait to hike with dad tomorrow. I can't believe I'm so close.

Day 107

Location: Katahdin Stream Campground

AT Mile: 2179.1

Miles Hiked Today With Dad: About 10

Dad and I got up around 5:30 am and left the hostel. Swung by McDonald's for breakfast and then headed to Abol Bridge where I was picked up from yesterday. From there we hiked to the base of Katahdin. The trail followed a river and we had to rock hop many large stream crossings. In the photo above we stopped to break at a small waterfall. The sun was out for most of the day and I welcomed it. I hadn't seen it for days through the 100 mile wilderness.

Our pace was slow but we made it to the campground around 2 pm. We registered at the ranger station and dad was able to secure a small lean-to for ourselves that somebody had called and canceled on. We were lucky because if we hadn't found something he would have either had to sleep in the car or drive back 19 miles to town. Baxter strictly enforces no stealth tenting. Thru hikers are allowed to stay at a shelter called The Birches for $10 on a first-come basis without reservations. Dad wouldn't have been allowed in though so I'm happy be we're able to get something else.

We left the park and drove back into town for dinner at the Appalachian Trail Cafe. A giant table of hikers were there who had just summited Katahdin today. Strange to think they are actually done and tomorrow I will be sitting in their shoes. Honey Badger was among them as well as a hiker named Sharky. I had seen his shark fin drawings in the shelter logs. He is 50 years old and doing what's called a yo-yo thru hike. This means he hiked the whole trail north like me but now he is preparing to hike all the way back to Georgia. Double dipping. The Appalachian Trail twice in one summer. Completely amazing. I hope he makes it.

Tomorrow morning we head up the Hunt Trail, also known as the AT. The end of the trail is only about five miles from here but over 4,000 feet of elevation gain is between us and Baxter Peak, the northern terminus of the AT. Thru hikers who have already finished have told me how hard this final climb is. We plan to take it very slow and begin at first light.

It hasn't set in yet that it's all about to end. I'm excited, I'm nervous, I'm happy, I'm overwhelmed… So many emotions are running through my mind. Tomorrow I finish the trail.

CHAPTER 5: KATAHDIN

Mt. Katahdin
Day 108
Northern Terminus of the Appalachian Trail
2,184.2 Miles Hiked
The end of the Journey

2,200 northbound thru hikers left GA this year. I was number 185 to finish.

I would like to dedicate my hike to my mother and father. My dad, who introduced me to the wilderness, taught me the meaning of hard work and to never give up. Also, my mom, who comforted me countless times during my trek and whose love and support kept me strong.

It was 108 days of blood, sweat, tears, rain, fog, rocks, mud, freeze dried dinners, electrical storms, mosquitoes, black flies, wet socks, hitch hiking, chafing, shelter mice, 30 degree temperatures, 100 degree temperatures and plenty of foot and joint pain. It was also 108 days of adventure, sunrises and sunsets, campfires surrounded by new friends, the sweet smells of a dense spruce forest, trail magic, gorgeous vistas, swimming in clear glacial lakes, eating everything I wanted and still losing weight, sleeping under the stars and knowing at every moment that I was doing something challenging, something incredible, something that would change my life.

It has been an incredible adventure. I lost 25 pounds. I saw 12 bears and a handful of venomous snakes. I had a mother bear confront me over her cub, had a mouse chew into my sleeping bag, hitch hiked on the back of a Harley Davidson, washed dishes for a place to sleep in huts and slept everywhere from the floors of churches and trail angel's homes to park pavilions, countless AT shelters and of course, my tent. I walked around laundry mats in a towel and rain jacket while my clothes washed and sat on many a convenience store corner devouring pints of ice cream. I'll be fine if I never see a granola bar ever again. I met some of the most interesting, amazingly inspirational people I've ever encountered on the trail and formed many strong friendships over the course of the trek. I learned a lot about myself, what I'm capable of and what I want out of life. I learned to appreciate the small things no matter how small and to always look at the glass half full. The trail helped me grow as an individual. I have become a better person because of it.

I passed every white blaze between Georgia and Maine. I never blue blazed, yellow blazed or slackpacked anything. For me that was the only way to approach the trail. Everyone should approach it in their own way.

I experienced both the happiest moment of my life and the mentally lowest point of my life on trail. It was by far the hardest thing I've ever accomplished. Still, I will miss it dearly; the community, the sense of freedom and the lifestyle that surrounded me for those few months.

I want to thank all of those who helped me along the way, whether it was giving me a ride somewhere, sharing food or water, helping me repair a piece of gear or even taking me in for the night. Your generosity has opened my eyes to how good people can be. I also want to thank all my friends and family back home who supported me and believed in me. Your encouragement helped me to stay strong.

If anyone is interested in thru hiking, planning an AT section hike, ultralight backpacking or looking for advice on cutting pack weight and would like to talk to me, you can get in touch with me by email at ryanjhouser@gmail.com or through @houserarchitecture on instagram.

For more information on the AT and ways to donate or volunteer, please visit www.appalachiantrail.org. The AT couldn't be what it is today without the many trail clubs and individuals that volunteer their time and resources.

Just remember: It's not about the miles, it's about the smiles!

ABOUT THE AUTHOR

Ryan Houser has lived in many locations but he particularly enjoys North Carolina, Colorado and South Korea. He has made countless frivolous life changes following his AT thru hike including but not limited to: thru hiking the Pacific Crest Trail in 2015, running a bunch of 50K and 50 mile trail races, working as a ski bum in Colorado, teaching English abroad in Asia, doing the whole Burning Man thing, working as a reporter, getting a masters in architecture and then wondering if that was a complete waste of time, driving a truck from North Carolina to Alaska (and back), and spending a year living the digital nomad life. It's possible that the AT ruined his professional career forever. He would still hike it every summer if he could.

Made in the USA
Monee, IL
10 December 2019